Jane Patrick &
Stephanie Flynn Sokolov

woven
scarves

26

Inspired Designs for the Rigid Heddle Loom

 INTERWEAVE.
interweave.com

Editor Ann Budd

Technical Editor Judy Steinkeonig

Associate Art Director Julia Boyles

Project Photographer Joe Hancock

Step Photographer Jane Patrick

Photo Stylist Emily Smoot

Hair and Makeup Jessica Shinyeda

Design Pamela Norman

Layout Julia Boyles

Production Katherine Jackson

Interweave
A division of F+W Media, Inc.
201 East Fourth Street
Loveland, CO 80537
interweave.com

Manufactured in China
by RR Donnelley Shenzhen

Library of Congress
Cataloging-in-Publication Data

Patrick, Jane.
Woven scarves : 26 inspired designs for
the rigid heddle loom / Jane
Patrick and Stephanie Flynn Sokolov.
     pages cm
Includes bibliographical references and
index.
ISBN 978-1-62033-119-4 (pbk.)
ISBN 978-1-62033-118-7 (PDF)
1. Hand weaving--Patterns. 2. Scarves.
I. Sokolov, Stephanie Flynn.
II. Title.
TT848.P424 2014
746.9'6--dc23

2013021762

10 9 8 7 6 5 4 3 2 1

Acknowledgments

We would like to thank all of our teachers, past and present, for instilling in us inspiration and confidence. This book would not have been possible without them. In addition, we would like to extend our appreciation to Interweave for having faith in us to publish this book. A special thank you to our editors, Ann Budd and Judy Steinkoenig.

We are most grateful to the following yarn companies for generously providing yarns for our projects: Alpaca with a Twist, Berroco, Brown Sheep, Classic Elite, Cotton Clouds, Imperial Stock Ranch, Koigu, Lorna's Laces, Louet North America, Mango Moon, Mountain Colors, North Light Fibers, Plymouth Yarn, Skacel, Tahki-Stacy Charles Inc., Trendsetter Yarns, and Universal Yarn.

We thank our Schacht intern Cei Lambert, who wove many samples and scarves. Also, thanks to Sara Goldberg White for her designs and Betty Paepke both for her design and for all of the weaving she did for us. We thank Margaret Tullis for her crochet expertise in writing the crochet instructions for the Peter Pan Collar. Thanks, too, to photographer Richard Cummings who did the step-by-step warping photography.

From Stephanie: I would like to thank my husband and family for giving me time and space to work. Also, a special thanks to Schacht Spindle Company for allowing me access to the finely crafted equipment used in this book. And finally, heartfelt thanks to my co-author, Jane. Her experience in the world of publishing and textiles has been invaluable. Her keen eye for detail and honesty has pushed me to be a better weaver. Thank you.

From Jane: This project just would not have happened without Stephanie. I don't think I've collaborated with another person quite so harmoniously. Stephanie has a wonderful sense of design, and I learned much from her creativity. Together, we were able to push our ideas and talents to create a wide range of pieces using only a simple rigid heddle loom. Many thanks to my husband, Barry Schacht, who tolerated my messes and the pressure of deadlines. In addition, I wouldn't have been able to devote as much time to this project if my staff at Schacht hadn't covered for me in my absences. Thanks to Kate, Denise, Judy, Gail, Rick, Nate, and Christy.

CONTENTS

INTRODUCTION

One of the best parts of being involved in weaving is the community of weavers. If you are new to weaving, then you may be just starting to meet other weavers. You'll find them to be generous, smart, creative, and passionate. It is a joy to work collaboratively with other weavers, and this is one of the reasons Stephanie Flynn Sokolov and I wanted to make this book together.

Stephanie and I met when she came to Schacht Spindle Company. I thought she was coming for an interview; she thought she was coming for a tour. The result: I hired Stephanie on the spot to be part of our sales team. We had a wonderful couple of years together, but then family and other priorities found Stephanie pursuing other interests. We kept in touch through other projects and, when I decided that a scarf book was what new enthusiastic weavers wanted, I immediately sought out Stephanie.

It's been an energizing partnership. Stephanie brings a keen design aesthetic, helped along no doubt by her training at the Fashion Institute of Technology in New York City. I have years of experience as writer, editor, and weaver. Our shared passion and the thrill of seeing ideas come to fruition have made creating this book together joyous.

Our goal for this book is to illustrate the broad range of possibilities weavers can attain with a simple rigid heddle loom. We chose to use the Cricket Loom from Schacht, with either a 10" (25.5 cm) or 15" (38 cm) weaving width (full disclosure:

I'm married to Schacht founder Barry Schacht and work alongside him as well . . . but still, it's a great little loom). This limited us to projects no wider than 15" (38 cm) and to warp setts of between 5 and 12 ends per inch (epi). Although these parameters have affected our choices, we think you'll be blown away with the incredible fabrics that such simple tools can create. The scarves in this collection prove that you can make amazing stuff on a simple loom.

We assume that you are a beginner or an advanced beginner weaver who has warped your loom several times and has woven a few projects. Although we designed all of these projects for the rigid heddle loom, we know that these projects will appeal to seasoned shaft loom weavers as well, and we have provided drafts where appropriate.

As references, we've provided warping instructions for direct peg warping (page 146) and measuring yarn on a warping board (page 151), a glossary of terms (page 156), and how to figure out how much yarn you have (page 154). Because yarns are always changing and may or may not be available when you're ready to weave one of the projects, we've included detailed yarn information with each project, which will go a long way in helping you make substitutions with confidence.

We hope that you love these scarf designs and that they inspire your own creative explorations.

—*Jane Patrick*

1 plain weave

The basic structure of most of the scarves in this book is plain weave. It's the simplest of weaves and the one most readily woven on a rigid heddle loom. In plain weave, every other warp thread (or end) is lifted—one up, one down, and so on. On the next pass of the weft, everything that was up is down and everything that was down is up. That is, every warp end that is raised on one pass is lowered on the next. These two passes are alternated to form an over, under, over, under interlacement of the warp and weft. However, even though the structure is simple, we like to say that there's nothing plain about plain weave. The scarves in this chapter are a case in point.

Balanced Weaves

In a balanced weave, there are the same number of warp ends as there are weft picks in 1" (2.5 cm) of woven cloth. The visual impact of warp and weft is about equal because each appears in the fabric in more or less the same amount. Keep in mind that you want your scarf to have a lot of drape. If you pack in the weft too tightly, you're likely to create a stiff fabric that won't provide the supple, drapey hand you want. For almost every scarf in this collection, we used balanced weaves to produce fabrics that wrap and drape beautifully.

When you weave a balanced weave with a single color in the warp and a single color in the weft, you'll want to consider how the colors mix visually. Let's say you cross a red warp with a blue weft in a balanced weave structure so that you'll have the same amount of each color. When you view the fabric at a distance, your eye will mix the colors to produce purple. This visual effect will be influenced by the size and color of the yarns, as well as the viewing distance. In weaving, the warp and weft will always influence each other, and you'll want to consider this influence when designing. You'll learn a lot if you weave a sample.

Stripes

Weaving naturally lends itself to stripes. It's easy to thread stripes in the warp and such lengthwise stripes are quite attractive on the wearer. Warp-wise stripes are a simple way to create pattern in weaving. All of the work is done in the warping process, and you need just one shuttle, which makes for speedy weaving. You can also add weft-wise stripes to create borders or broad horizontal stripes. Weaving weft stripes has the advantage that the pattern can be changed at any time— an advantage over warp stripes, which can't be altered once the loom is threaded.

When you design striped warps, keep in mind that if you work in patterns with even numbers, you can use the efficient direct peg warping method (see page 146). When you warp odd numbers, it's probably best to measure the warp on the warping board, then thread the heddle according to the pattern. Theoretically, you can thread the heddle in pairs and then move ends around in the reed afterwards, but we've fumbled through some weaving frustrations when yarns became twisted behind the heddle. It wasn't fun. Also, if some warp ends are crossed over others for too long a distance, you can run into problems weaving, especially as you approach the end of the warp.

Tips for Designing Stripes

- ► A single end of a contrasting color forms a dotted line.
- ► Two ends threaded together with broad stripes of solid colors on each side act as a pinstripe.
- ► If you want single colors to follow the same pattern, you need to thread them all the same way—in either slots or holes.
- ► Use yarn wrappings to explore stripe ideas, especially for unbalanced stripe designs.
- ► Draw your stripe pattern on paper before you warp the loom.
- ► For balanced patterns, make sure that the same color is at each selvedge.

Checks and Plaids

Crossing a striped warp with weft stripes creates a plaid or check that's ultimately appealing and well suited to woven designs. Once you start looking, you'll find plaids and checks all around—in interior fabrics, coats, skirts, and flannel shirts. All are ready inspiration for scarves.

Despite many years of weaving, we still find the different patterns created by simple changes in the color interlacement magical. The structure is always the same, over, under, over, under, but the color order creates a pattern that looks like so much more. The Log Cabin Scarf (page 22), a color-and-weave pattern, is a case in point.

Generally, when you design color-and-weave patterns, you cross no more than one or two (or sometimes three or four) warp ends to create the pattern. If you study the variations for our Chunky Check Scarf (page 8), you'll see that patterns are created just by changing how the colors are woven.

If you think of weaving as if it were a computer with Xs and Os (the thread is either "off" or "on"), you can start to visualize how color-and-weave works. A thread can be only up or down. That is, sometimes the thread is raised to the surface where you can see it; other times, it's hidden beneath a weft that crosses it.

An example of color-and-weave effect is the log cabin pattern. In this technique, two colors are alternated in both the warp and weft. The unique pattern appears as you simply repeat a color twice, which shifts the interlacement of the colors. You'll see in our Log Cabin Scarf (page 22) that sometimes the stripes are horizontal in one block, but vertical in the next block. The shift occurs at the point where a color is repeated. So, a log cabin pattern might be threaded A, B, A, B, A, B, B, A, B, A, B, A, with the pattern shifting at the point where B is repeated.

For log cabin, the weft color order generally follows the way that the warp is threaded. Traditionally, the same colors are used in warp and weft.

Tips for Designing Checks and Plaids

- ► The yarn colors must contrast enough for the pattern to show up.
- ► A balanced weave is best.
- ► You can use different yarns in the weft, but they'll need to have some contrast for the pattern to appear.
- ► Introduce texture by alternating, for example, a fuzzy yarn with a smooth yarn.
- ► You can use spaced-dyed yarns as long as the colors contrast enough.

The combination of yarn, sett, and weave work together to weave up this classy check that is cloud-soft and a great first project for weaving with two shuttles.

CHUNKY CHECK

If you visualize gingham fabric, you have an idea of a check. Generally, a check is created by alternating equal widths of two colors in the warp and weaving the weft in the same color sequence as threaded in the warp. The simple delight of this pattern is the balancing of solid squares with blended squares where the two contrasting colors cross. This Chunky Check Scarf is a wonderful example of a simple check that weaves up quickly at 5 epi. The yarn is a dreamy chainette that's soft and squishy—perfect for a scarf.

Designed by Stephanie Flynn Sokolov | *Woven by* Betty Paepke

Finished size: 7" (18 cm) wide and 80" (203 cm) long, plus 6" (15 cm) fringe at each end.

Structure: Plain weave.

Equipment: 10" (25.5 cm) wide, 5-dent rigid heddle loom; two stick shuttles; tapestry needle.

Yarn: *Classic Elite Yarns MountainTop Chalet* (70% alpaca, 30% bamboo at 896 yd/lb [819 m/453 g] in #7416 Parchment (warp and weft): 135 yd (2 skeins at 98 yd [90 m]/50 g); and #7477 Charcoal (warp and weft): 120 yd (2 skeins).

Warp length: 110" (279.5 cm), which allows 18" (45.5 cm) for loom waste and includes 12" (30.5 cm) for fringe—6" (15 cm) at each end.

Total warp ends: 44.

Width in reed: About 9" (23 cm).

Ends per inch: 5.

Picks per inch: 5.

Yarn Wrapping

This is shown actual size to assist you in making substitutions. Just place the yarn you want to use on top of the yarn chart to see if the yarn is the same size. Substituting a yarn with similar fiber content will be most successful.

top to bottom:

➤ Classic Elite Yarns MountainTop Chalet in Charcoal.

➤ Classic Elite Yarns MountainTop Chalet in Parchment.

Warping

Using the direct peg technique (see page 146) and following the warping plan below, sley 2 slots of Parchment, skip 2 slots, sley 2 slots of Parchment, and so on, until 24 threads have been measured. Then fill in the unthreaded slots with Charcoal for a total of 20 ends.

Warping Plan

	Repeat 5 times		End	
Parchment	4		4	24
Charcoal		4		20
Total Ends				**44**

Weaving

Wind Parchment and Charcoal on separate stick shuttles.

Allow sufficient length in your front tie-on for a 6" (15 cm) fringe.

Leaving a tail four times the weaving width for hemstitching, weave 6 picks with Parchment.

Use the tail to hemstitch (see page 153) over 4 warp ends and 2 weft picks.

Weave a balanced weave at 5 ppi, alternating 4 picks of Charcoal and 4 picks of Parchment and using a light hand to beat the weaving to square, checking often to ensure that the weaving is balanced. Weave as far as you can.

The fabric on the loom will look quite open but will full up during the finishing process.

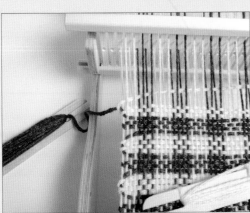

▲ For this scarf, we carried the nonactive shuttle up the selvedge, catching the yarn with the active shuttle. Alternately, you can cut off the yarn at each color change, but the ends will need to be woven or sewn in. With a yarn this bulky, weaving in the ends will create extra bulk at the selvedges and interrupt the pleasant weft patterning at the edges.

▲ Chunky Check Scarf on loom. The weave will look very open. To ensure a balanced weave, be sure that the spaces between the yarns form little squares.

Finish with 6 rows of Parchment, then hemstitch over 4 warps and 2 wefts.

Note: *In general, the main challenge of weaving checks is to create a balanced weave. The best way to do this is to be sure that the spaces at the intersections of the threads are square. It's a good idea as well to measure your weft picks when the warp is off tension. Simply release the brake so that the warp relaxes, then check the "square" of the weaving and adjust your beat accordingly. Doing so is particularly important if you're weaving with a very stretchy yarn.*

Finishing

To remove the fabric from the loom, cut as close to the back apron rod as possible. Untie the front knots to allow for the fringe.

Handwash in hot water with a small amount of Dawn or a similar detergent.

Rinse in warm water.

If the scarf is not sufficiently fulled, place it in the dryer set on medium heat, checking every 5 minutes until desired hand is achieved.

Lay flat to dry.

Steam-press.

Trim fringe to 6" (15 cm) using a rotary cutter or scissors.

making color changes

When you weave with more than one weft color, you can choose how to end one color and begin the next. One option is to cut off the yarn that's ending, weave the tail into the shed for a little way, then begin the next color, securing the end in the shed as well. This technique can take quite a bit of time if you have many color changes. It can also build up the edges if the yarn is thick, and the tails can create a thick area at each color change that will affect the overall lines of the weave to its detriment.

Because the yarns are thick and the color changes often at every fifth pick, we chose to carry the weft not in use up the selvedge. The active shuttle "catches" the loose weft as it enters the shed for the next row. This technique is a bit slower than weaving with just one shuttle, but it's faster than starting and stopping at each color change. We found that the yarn carried up the selvedge did not affect the overall check design. To alternate the wefts traveling up the selvedges, we started the shuttles on the opposite sides of the scarf, one beginning from right to left and the other beginning from left toright.

Variations

We wove five variations on the same warp, as follows:

➤ Solid gray weft.

➤ Alternate two white and two gray wefts.

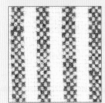

➤ Solid white weft.

➤ Alternate one white and one gray weft.

➤ Alternate three gray and one white weft.

Designed by Jane Patrick

This sporty scarf, sett at 5 epi, would be perfect paired with a leather jacket or a sweater knitted with the same yarns. The shifting colors of the accent yarn contribute to the overall charm of the windowpane plaid. It weaves up in a jiffy, too.

WINDOWPANE PLAID

A windowpane plaid is another way to cross warp and weft to create a pattern. A solid background sectioned off by narrow warp and weft stripes creates little "windows," or the windowpane plaid. For this example, the blocks are of equal size and just two yarns are used to weave a simple pattern. You can, though, interpret this idea many ways: you could use different warp and weft yarns or you could try blocks of unequal sizes, as long as the windows are delineated with crisscrossing lines of warp and weft.

Designed and woven by Sara Goldenberg White

Finished size: 5¾" (14.5 cm) wide and 65" (165 cm) long, plus 2" (5 cm) fringe at each end.

Structure: Plain weave.

Equipment: 10" (25.5 cm) wide, 5-dent rigid heddle reed; two stick shuttles; tapestry needle.

Yarn: *Berroco Remix* (30% nylon, 27% cotton, 24% acrylic, 10% silk, 9% linen at 987 yd/lb [902 m/453 g]) in #3924 Clementine (warp and weft): 150 yd (1 skein at 206 yd [188 m]/100 g).

Berroco Boboli (42% wool, 35% acrylic, 23% viscose at 941 yd/lb [860 m/453 g]) in #5329 Jammie (warp and weft): 80 yd (1 skein at 206 yd [188 m]/100 g).

Warp length: 98" (249 cm), which allows 18" (45.5 cm) for loom waste and includes 4" (10 cm) for fringe—2" (5 cm) at each end.

Total warp ends: 35.

Width in reed: 7" (18 cm).

Ends per inch: 5.

Picks per inch: 8.

Yarn Wrapping

This yarn wrapping is shown actual size to assist you in making substitutions. Just place the yarn you want to use on top of the yarn chart to see if the yarn is the same size. Substituting a yarn with similar fiber content will be most successful.

Top to bottom:

➤ Berroco Remix in #3924 Clementine.
➤ Berroco Boboli in #5329 Jammie.

Warping

Use the indirect method of measuring the warp on a warping board (see page 151), following the warping plan below.

Warping Plan

	Repeat 4 times		End	
Boboli	3		3	15
Remix		5		20
	Total Ends			**35**

Weaving

Wind Boboli and Remix on separate stick shuttles.

Leave at least 2" (5 cm) of space from the apron rod to allow for fringe.

Leaving a tail about four times the weaving width for hemstitching, weave 2 picks of Boboli.

Use the tail to hemstitch (see page 153) over 2 warp ends and 2 weft picks.

Weave 1 more pick of Boboli, then alternate 8 picks Remix and 3 picks Boboli until the scarf measures 70" (178 cm) or as far as the warp length will allow, weaving in the tails as you go.

Hemstitch with Boboli over 2 warps and 2 wefts.

Note: *When you change yarns, alternate sides so that the tails are not all woven in on the same side (which could cause your weaving to build up more on one side than the other).*

Finishing

Remove the scarf from the loom, cutting as close to the apron rod as possible to allow for fringe.

Handwash in warm soapy water, agitating the fabric to full it.

Rinse in cool water and lay flat to dry.

Trim fringe to 2" (5 cm).

If needed, steam-press using a pressing cloth.

Variation

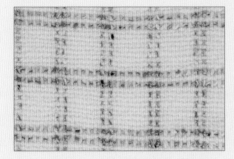

➤ This fabric has a solid white warp and weft accented by a novelty yarn that's separated in the warp and weft by a single white yarn. Even though the outlining yarns aren't right next to each other, they still read as a windowpane. When threaded in this way, the accent yarn follows the same over, under path. Yarns are Brown Sheep Nature Spun Sport Weight in #740 Snow and Filatura di Crosa Tempo in #8 Northern Lights (this color has been discontinued; you can substitute #43 Scarlet Fever) woven at 10 epi and 10 ppi.

Designed by Jane Patrick

This simple piece is woven from a soft alpaca-blend yarn with single-end accents in a heavier-weight merino wool. Handsome and professional looking, this scarf is great for both men and women. Pair it with a black pea coat, simple dress shirt, or black sweater for an off-Fifth Avenue sense of style—or dress it down as shown here.

GO TO WORK

This is an easy first project for learning to measure the warp on the warping board. We like to use a warping board for this type of project because there are single warp ends spaced out across the warp. It's impractical to move the warp threads to accommodate the warp color order pattern, so we measured each yarn separately, then sleyed them in the heddle according to the pattern. Alternatively, you could change the single-end accent strips to pairs of warps and use the direct method of warping. But you wouldn't get the nice little dots that result from single ends.

Designed and woven by Cei Lambert

Finished size: 7" (18 cm) wide and 66" (168 cm) long, plus about 1" (2.5 cm) fringe at each end.

Structure: Plain weave.

Equipment: 10" (25.5 cm) wide, 10-dent rigid heddle reed; one stick shuttle; tapestry needle.

Yarn: *Alpaca with a Twist Socrates* (30% alpaca, 30% merino, 20% bamboo, 20% nylon at 1,828 yd/lb [603 m/453 g]) in #0403 Charcoal (warp and weft): 175 yd for warp and 165 yd for weft (1 skein at 400 yd [365 m]/100 g).

Alpaca with a Twist Highlander (45% merino, 45% alpaca, 8% microfiber, 2% nylon at 650 yd/lb [693 m/453 g]) in #3016 Tartan Red (warp only): 20 yd (1 skein at 144 yd [132 m]/100 g).

Warp length: 90" (229 cm), which allows 18" (45.5 cm) for loom waste and includes 2" (5 cm) for fringe—1" (2.5 cm) at each end.

Total warp ends: 78.

Width in reed: 7¾" (19.5 cm).

Ends per inch: 10.

Picks per inch: 10.

Yarn Wrapping

This yarn wrapping is shown actual size to assist you in making substitutions. Just place the yarn you want to use on top of the yarn chart to see if the yarn is the same size. Substituting a yarn with similar fiber content will be most successful.

Top to bottom:

➤ Alpaca with a Twist Socrates in #0403 Charcoal.

➤ Alpaca with a Twist Highlander in #3016 Tartan Red.

Warping

Use the indirect method of measuring the warp on a warping board (see page 151), following the warping plan below.

Warping Plan

Highlander	1		1		1		1		1		1		1		1	8
Socrates		10		10		10		10		10		10		10		70
	Total Ends															**78**

Weaving

Because the accent yarn is threaded along the selvedges, you'll want to maintain an even beat and tidy edges.

Wind Socrates on the stick shuttle.

Leave at least 1" (2.5 cm) of space from the apron rod to allow for fringe.

Leaving a tail four times the weaving width for hemstitching, weave 2 picks.

Use the tail to hemstitch (see page 153) over 2 warp ends and 2 weft picks.

Weave at 10 ppi, paying attention to maintain even edges that don't disrupt the contrasting color stripe at each selvedge, until scarf measures 70" (178 cm).

Hemstitch over 2 warps and 2 wefts.

Finishing

Remove the fabric from the loom, cutting as close to the apron rod as possible to allow for fringe.

Handwash in very warm water and mild detergent and rinse in warm water.

Lay flat to dry.

Steam-press with firm pressure. Trim fringe to about 1" (2.5 cm).

Bulky-weight yarns in two colors are sett at 5 epi for a scarf that weaves up quickly. The pattern is created by a color-and-weave technique called log cabin. You could think of this weave as a block pattern, with the first block threaded dark, light, dark, light and the second block threaded light, dark, light, dark. It's woven in the same sequence as it's threaded.

LOG CABIN

Log cabin is a bold color-and-weave technique that always looks like a complicated weave structure when, in fact, it's just plain weave. What causes the pattern is the interaction of the warp color order and the weft color order. Traditionally, log cabin is woven in two alternating colors, threaded dark, light, dark, light, for example. The shift happens when a color is repeated, such as light, light, dark, light, dark, light, and so on. The pattern changes because what was up is now down and the color that appeared on the surface becomes hidden underneath. Weaving proceeds just like the warp color order, with two colors alternating and then shifting to change the pattern. Try it! You'll see.

Designed by Jane Patrick and Stephanie Flynn Sokolov | **Woven by** Stephanie Flynn Sokolov

Finished size: 11½" (29 cm) wide and 82" (208 cm) long, plus 8" (20.5 cm) fringe at each end.

Structure: Plain weave with log cabin color-and-weave effect.

Equipment: 15" (38 cm) wide, 5-dent rigid heddle reed; two 15" (38 cm) stick shuttles; fringe twister (optional).

Yarn: Classic Elite MountainTop Blackthorn (50% wool, 50% superfine alpaca at 545 yd/lb [498 m/453 g]) in #7003 Ash (warp and weft): 200 yd (2 skeins at 120 yd [109 m]/100 g) and #7077 Seal (warp and weft): 210 yd (2 skeins).

Warp length: 120" (305 cm), which allows 24" (61 cm) for loom waste and includes 16" (40.5 cm) for fringe—8" (20.5) at each end.

Total warp ends: 70.

Width in reed: 14" (35.5 cm).

Ends per inch: 5.

Picks per inch: 5.

Yarn Wrapping

This yarn wrapping is shown actual size to assist you in making substitutions. Just place the yarn you want to use on top of the yarn chart to see if the yarn is the same size. Substituting a yarn with similar fiber content will be most successful.

Top to bottom:

➤ Classic Elite MountainTop Blackthorn in #7077 Seal.

➤ Classic Elite MountainTop Blackthorn in #7003 Ash.

Warping

We suggest measuring the two colors together on the warping board (see page 151). If you use the direct warping technique (see page 146) instead, you'll need to thread a light slot then a dark slot all the way across the reed and then adjust the threading of the holes to follow the color pattern. Because you'd be taking the yarns out of the reed and moving them around, the threads will become crossed behind the heddle and could cause some stickiness in the weaving.

Thread the blocks: A, B, A, B, A for a total of 5 blocks using the following color sequences where L = Ash and D = Seal.

Block A: L D L D L D L D L D L D L D

Block B: D L D L D L D L D L D L D L

Weaving

Wind Ash (L) on one stick shuttle and Seal (D) on the other.

Leave at least 8" (20.5 cm) of space from the apron rod to allow for fringe.

Leaving a tail four times the weaving width for hemstitching, weave 2 picks of dark yarn.

Weave Block A, alternating picks of light, dark, light, dark until 14 total picks (7 of each color) have been woven, ending with a dark yarn.

Use the dark tail to hemstitch (see page 153) over 2 warp ends and 2 weft picks.

Weave Block B, starting with a dark yarn followed by a light yarn. Repeat this dark-light sequence seven times for a total of 14 picks.

making a twisted fringe with a fringe twister

Making a twisted fringe tames and gives bulk to the warp fringe and adds a "finished" look to the scarf. To make a twisted fringe, twist two warp yarns or two sets of yarns in the direction of the yarn twist. You can figure out which way to twist by just testing a warp thread to see which way adds more twist and which way takes out twist.

The first step in making a twisted fringe is over twisting the yarns in one direction—the direction that adds more twist—then twisting them back in the opposite direction to twist the yarns together. A knot tied at the end keeps the yarns from untwisting.

Although you can do the twisting with your fingers, it takes awhile, especially if the yarns are fine. We used a fringe twister, which is a handy tool that speeds the process exponentially.

Step 1. Using one dark and one light warp yarn per (hemstitched) group, attach a light thread onto one clip and a dark thread onto the other. Clipping each yarn at an equal distance from the end of the scarf will help make an evenly twisted fringe.

Twist in the direction of the twist in the yarn. In this case, we twisted to the right. For a uniform look to the fringe, count thirty turns of the fringe twister for each group.

Step 2. Remove the yarns from the twister and hold them together. Do not let go of the yarns or they'll untwist.

Step 3. Tie an overhand knot and let go of the yarns to allow them to twist back in the other direction. Adjust the knots to the same length. Trim the ends.

Step 1

Step 2

Step 3

Variations

➤ Variation 1: For this variation, we alternated Brick and Curry in blocks of equal size in the warp. We then alternated short and long blocks in the weft. Yarn is Universal Yarns Nettie Lana sett at 5 epi.

➤ Variation 2: Two very thick novelty yarns were threaded and woven in equal-sized blocks. The texture of the yarns creates a fuzzy, irregular surface. Yarns are Sensation Angel Hair (#650 Beige and #4729 Dark Brown) sett at 5 epi.

Designed by Stephanie Flynn Sokolov

Alternate Block A and Block B until the scarf measures 90" (228.5 cm).

Weave 2 picks of dark yarn.

Hemstitch with dark yarn over 2 warps and 2 wefts.

Notes: *When the blocks shift, you'll have 2 rows of the same color next to each other (this will help you keep track of which block you're on if you take a break from weaving).*

When you alternate two shuttles of different colors, you'll need to catch the warp yarn at the edge of the weaving. You can do so by the way that you place the shuttle into the shed. Notice that one shuttle travels over the other at one selvedge and then under the other at the other selvedge. Because there are two picks of the same color at block changes, you'll want to adjust how the two shuttles interact at the edges.

If you want your scarf to end and begin on the same block, make a note of how you started so that you can repeat the same sequence at the other end.

Finishing

Remove the scarf from the loom, cutting as close to the apron rod as possible to allow for fringe.

Twist fringe as described on page 25.

Handwash in warm soapy water, agitating the fabric to full it.

Rinse in cool water and lay flat to dry.

If needed, steam-press using a pressing cloth.

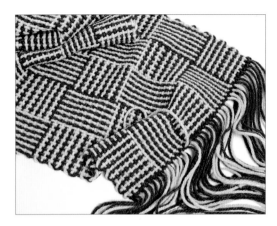

▲ *The woven scarf before washing and fringe twisting.*

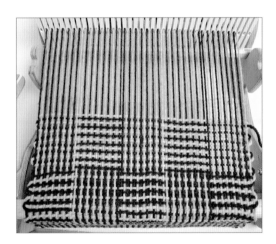

▲ *The log cabin scarf on the loom.*

Cuddly and cozy, this bouncy scarf is one you'll wear day after day. Because it's woven with a crepe yarn that has a lot of spring, this fabric has a soft drape that makes it so, so comfortable. It's fast and easy to weave, too.

SKWOOSH

For many of the scarves in this book, the way that they're finished is key to their final look and feel. Different fiber contents and yarn constructions affect how yarns behave in the finishing process. Wool and other animal fibers such as alpaca and mohair will full to the point of felting. Heavy fulling is needed to bring this scarf to its full beauty, but going too far will felt the yarn and make the fabric too dense and stiff. Fulling fabric isn't rocket science, but it does require vigilance. When you're in the process of fulling a fabric, especially when you use a washing machine or a dryer, pay close attention. Resist the temptation to make a phone call, load the dishwasher, or check your email. Five minutes can ruin a fabric. We know this from painful experience.

Designed and woven by Stephanie Flynn Sokolov

Finished size: 9½" (24 cm) wide and 66" (167.5 cm) long, plus 5" (12.5 cm) fringe at each end.

Structure: Plain weave.

Equipment: 15" (38 cm) wide, 8-dent rigid heddle reed; one stick shuttle; tapestry needle; fringe twister (optional).

Yarn: *Mountain Colors Twizzle* (85% merino, 15% silk at 1,136 yd/lb [1,038 m/453 g]) in Wild Horse (warp only): 205 yd (1 skein at 250 yd [228 m]/100 g).

Mountain Colors Merino Ribbon (80% superfine merino, 20% nylon at 980 yd/lb [896 m/453 g]) in Peppergrass (warp only): 60 yd (1 skein at 630 yd [576 m]/170 g).

Mountain Colors Half Crepe (100% merino wool at 1,680 yd/lb [1,536 m/453 g]) in Larkspur (warp and weft): 295 yd (2 skeins at 245 yd [224 m]/113 g).

Warp length: 102" (259 cm), which allows 24" (61 cm) for loom waste and includes 12" (30.5 cm) for fringe—6" (15 cm) at each end.

Total warp ends: 111.

Width in reed: 13¾" (35 cm).

Ends per inch: 8.

Picks per inch: 7.

Yarn Wrapping

This yarn wrapping is shown actual size to assist you in making substitutions. Just place the yarn you want to use on top of the yarn chart to see if the yarn is the same size. Substituting a yarn with similar fiber content will be most successful.

Top to bottom:

➤ Mountain Colors Twizzle in Wild Horse.
➤ Mountain Colors Merino Ribbon in Peppergrass.
➤ Mountain Colors Half Crepe in Larkspur.

Warping

Use the indirect method to measure the warp on a warping board (see page 151), winding 71 ends of Twizzle, 20 ends of Merino Ribbon, and 20 ends of Half Crepe, following the warping plan below.

Warping Plan

			Repeat 10 times				
Twizzle	2*	6				9*	71
Merino Ribbon				1	1		20
Half Crepe			1	1			20
Total Ends							111

*Begin and end in a slot

Weaving

Wind Half Crepe on the stick shuttle.

Leave at least 6" (15 cm) of space from the apron rod to allow for fringe.

Leaving a tail four times the weaving width for hemstitching, weave 3 picks, beating firmly to compact them together.

Use the tail to hemstitch (see page 153) over 2 warp ends and 3 weft picks.

Weave at 7 ppi, checking your beat periodically to maintain a consistent beat, until scarf measures 78" (198 cm).

Hemstitch over 2 warps and 3 wefts.

Notes: *Wind the shuttle with very little tension to prevent stretching the yarn.*

The stretchy, springy Half Crepe yarn requires a little attention at the selvedges. For smooth edges, adjust the yarn to make sure it "turns the corner" at the edges. Instead of pulling the yarn through

the shed, lay it in at a 30-degree angle so that it has plenty of freedom to move around. Doing so prevents excessive draw-in and lets the yarn stretch later on in the fabric.

Finishing

Remove the fabric from the loom, cutting as close to the apron rod as possible to allow for fringe.

Handwash in hot water with a little agitation.

Place the scarf and a dark towel in the dryer for 20 minutes on the low setting. Check often to monitor the fulling process. The scarf is finished when the weave structure is no longer apparent; if you can see the square holes between the warp and weft, put it back in the dryer for 5 minutes at a time. This yarn hits a "flash point" at which it will suddenly felt. You don't want to cross that threshold and over-full the scarf, because there's no going back. Checking often is key.

Lightly steam-press with little pressure so as not to compress the fabric. Use your fingers to hold sections of the fringe and press down hard on the fringe with the iron to straighten it.

Make twisted fringe (see page 25) on groups of 4 ends. Tie each group into an overhand knot 5" (12.5 cm) from the hemstitching. Trim the ends.

Note: *Draw-in occurs on almost all weaving. The yarn you use and the way it's tensioned as you wind it on the shuttle can affect the amount of draw-in. When you weave, you also need to consider take-up. The kind of yarn, weave structure, and the finishing process all affect take-up. For this project, because of the nature of the yarn and the finishing process, the shrinkage and take-up were around 20 percent.*

Variation

➤ Similar yarns from Mountain Colors were used to weave this variation in a fall blaze colorway. In the warp, three colors of Twizzle, Trading Post, Yellowstone, and Ruby River were used along with accents of Merino Ribbon in Harmony Garnet and Winter Lace in Indian Paintbrush. The weft is Half Crepe in Trading Post. No particular color order was used for this scarf. Yarns were measured on the warping board and then threaded randomly in the reed for a rich blend of color and texture. The wool crepe weft gives the fabric bounce.

Designed and woven by Cei Lambert

This muffler is generously oversized and could be dressed up or down. The worsted-weight wool yarn is soft and warm, and it weaves and finishes beautifully.

PLAID MUFFLER

Woven plaids consist of rectangles of overlapping colors that are appealing to both weave and wear. This asymmetrical oversized plaid is a bit unconventional, featuring a nonrepeating pattern instead of the more expected balanced plaid from selvedge to selvedge. The long pattern repeat in the weft is woven in reverse to produce a muffler that's symmetrical from end to end but that appears to be nonrepeating. For the most pleasing plaids, try to maintain an even beat throughout the weaving.

Designed and woven by Stephanie Flynn Sokolov

Finished size: 11" (28 cm) wide and 76" (193 cm) long, plus 6" (15 cm) fringe at each end.

Structure: Plain weave.

Equipment: 15" (38 cm) wide, 8-dent rigid heddle reed; four stick shuttles; tapestry needle; rotary cutter; healing mat.

Yarn: *Imperial Stock Ranch Tracie Too 2-ply Sport* (100% merino wool at 1,580 yd/ lb [1,444 m/453 g]: available in skeins of 395 yd [361 m]/113 g) in the following colors (all in both warp and weft):

◆ #351 Autumn Rust: 36 yd (1 skein at 395 yd [362 m]/113 g)

◆ #314 Chocolate 130 yd (1 skein)

◆ #315 Wild Rye: 90 yd (1 skein)

◆ #326 Denim Dusk: 355 yd (1 skein).

Warp length: 109" (277 cm), which allows 24" (61 cm) for loom waste and includes 12" (30.5 cm) for fringe—6" (15 cm) at each end.

Total warp ends: 112.

Width in reed: 14" (35.5 cm).

Ends per inch: 8.

Picks per inch: 7.

Yarn Wrapping

This yarn wrapping is shown actual size to assist you in making substitutions. Just place the yarn you want to use on top of the yarn chart to see if the yarn is the same size. Substituting a yarn with similar fiber content will be most successful.

Top to bottom:

➤ Imperial Stock Ranch 2-ply Sport in #314 Chocolate.

➤ Imperial Stock Ranch 2-ply Sport in #315 Wild Rye.

➤ Imperial Stock Ranch 2-ply Sport in #326 Denim Dusk.

➤ Imperial Stock Ranch 2-ply Sport in #351 Autumn Rust.

Warping

Using the direct peg method (page 146), follow the warping plan below.

Warping Plan

Denim	26						20				14	60
Chocolate		8		8		8			4			28
Rust			4		4							8
Rye								8		8		16
Total Ends												**112**

Weaving

Wind each color on a separate stick shuttle.

Allow sufficient length in your front tie-on for a 6" (15 cm) fringe. Leaving a tail four times the weaving width for hemstitching, weave 3 picks of Denim.

Use the tail to hemstitch (see page 153) over 3 warp ends and 3 weft picks.

Weave according to the weft sequence on page 37, cutting the yarn after each color band. To do this neatly, place the tail of the yarn over the first up warp thread on the side where the shuttle enters the shed and place it under the next 2 up threads in the same shed as the first pick. When the section of color is completed and the open shed contains the last thread of the patterning sequence, cut off the yarn and place it over the first up thread, then under the next 2 up threads in the same shed. Beat in these first and last wefts with the same beat, being careful that the ends are overlapping in the section of the same color. When the colors are contained within each color block, your eye is not as likely to notice that the first and last picks are slightly uneven.

Hemstitch with Denim over 3 warps and 3 wefts.

▲ The fabric will look very open before washing but will full during the finishing process.

▲ The ends are trimmed flush with the surface of the fabric after fulling.

Weft Sequence

Denim	26						54				20				20				54			
Chocolate		8		8		8			4				4				4				8		8*
Rust			4		4																	4	
Rye								8		8		8		8		8		8					

Reverse the sequence of the pattern starting with the 4 rust, 8 chocolate, 54 denim, and so on.

Note: *Because this yarn is fairly elastic, we adjusted our weaving to prevent excessive draw-in at the selvedges. Give plenty of angle to your weft in the shed and use a light tension when you pull the weft through the shed.*

Finishing

Remove the fabric from the loom, cutting as close to the apron rod as possible to allow for fringe.

Tie the fringe in bundles of 6 warp ends with overhand knots.

Handwash in warm water.

Place the scarf and a towel in the dryer on the low setting and check every 5 minutes until yarn is fluffy and the individual threads appear blurred.

Steam-press on warm setting.

Trim all of the ends left from color changes.

Gently brush the fringe to straighten it, then press it and trim it to 6" (15 cm), using a ruler and rotary cutter on a healing mat.

Variation

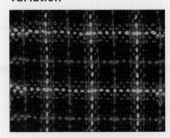

➤ It can be completely satisfying to design and weave a small, simple plaid like this one, which uses the same yarns as those used for the project scarf. Because of the many color changes, the yarns were snipped and woven into the web for ½" (1.3 cm) or less. The yarn tails were left hanging until after washing, then clipped flush with the surface of the fabric. Leaving the tails uncut until after washing lets the yarns full, which makes the ends less apt to work loose.

Designed and woven by Cei Lambert

Warping and Weaving Color Order

	Repeat 3x									Total Ends
Denim				2		2				12
Chocolate	4		4				4		4	32
Rust		1								3
Rye					1			1		4
Total Ends										51

By their very nature, pom-poms are lighthearted and lend play to a design. They're used in a casual way here, but could also be given sophisticated appeal. Think many tiny white pom-poms on the ends of an all-white scarf.

BOBBLE SCARF

Here's a scarf that's sure to draw attention. The self-striping novelty accent yarn lends a dynamic element to the otherwise plain fabric. The ends of the scarf are punctuated with plaid borders and jumpy, jazzy pom-poms. We guarantee that this delightful piece will be fun to make and wear.

Designed and woven by Stephanie Flynn Sokolov

Finished size: 7" (18 cm) wide and 57" (145 cm) long, plus 4" (10 cm) fringe and pom-poms at each end.

Structure: Plain weave.

Equipment: 10" (25.5 cm) wide, 10-dent rigid heddle reed; three stick shuttles; pom-pom maker; sharp scissors; tapestry needle.

Yarn: *Skacel/Fil Royal* (100% baby alpaca at 3,017 yd/lb [2,758 m/453 g]) in the following colors:

◆ #3509 9259 Gold (warp and weft): 347 yd (1 skein at 660 yd [604 m]/100 g)

◆ #3515 9265 Royal Blue (weft only): 3 yd (1 skein).

Skacel/HiKoo Timidity (40% wool, 43% acrylic, 17% nylon at 2,240 yd/lb [2,048 m/453 g]) in #3 Red (warp and weft): 55 yd (1 skein at 245 yd [224 m]/50 g).

Note: Additional yarn is required for the pom-poms.

Warp length: 90" (228.5 cm), which allows 24" (61 cm) for loom waste and includes 8" (20.5 cm) for fringe—4" (10 cm) at each end.

Total warp ends: 90.

Width in reed: 9" (23 cm).

Ends per inch: 10.

Picks per inch: 10.

Yarn Wrapping

This yarn wrapping is shown actual size to assist you in making substitutions. Just place the yarn you want to use on top of the yarn chart to see if the yarn is the same size. Substituting a yarn with similar fiber content will be most successful.

Top to bottom:

➤ Skacel/Fil Royal in #3509 9259 Gold.

➤ Skacel/Fil Royal in #3515 9265 Royal Blue.

➤ Skacel/HiKoo Timidity in #3 Red.

Warping

Use the direct peg method (page 146), starting with Fil Royal in gold, beginning in the fourth slot from the edge of the heddle, and following the warping plan below.

Warping Plan

		Repeat 9 times		
Fil Royal (gold)	8	6	8	70
Timidity		2	2	20
				90

Weaving

Wind each yarn on a separate stick shuttle, noting that majority of the scarf is woven with Fil Royal in Gold.

Allow sufficient length in your front tie-on for 6" (15 cm) fringe and pom-pom. Leaving a tail four times the weaving width for hemstitching, weave 2 picks with Fil Royal in Gold. Beat these 2 picks to compact them together, then use the tail to hemstitch (see page 153) over 2 warp ends and 2 weft picks.

Weave 28 more picks of Fil Royal in Gold.

For the border plaid, weave 2 picks Timidity, 3 picks Fil Royal in Gold, 2 picks Fil Royal in Blue, 3 picks Fil Royal in Gold, 2 picks Timidity, 3 picks Fil Royal in Gold, 2 picks Fil Royal in Blue, 3 picks Fil Royal in Gold, and 2 picks Timidity.

Weave in Fil Royal in Gold for 55" (139.5 cm).

Weave another border plaid as before.

Weave 28 picks of Fil Royal in Gold.

Hemstitch with Fil Royal in Gold over 2 warps and 2 wefts.

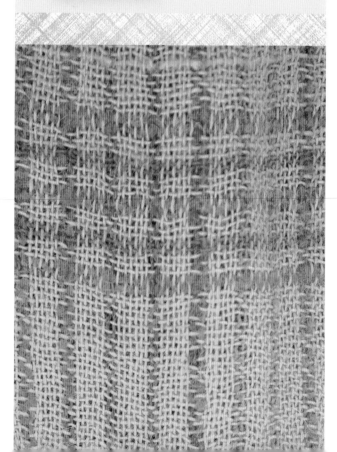

Finishing

Remove the fabric from the loom, cutting as close to the apron rod as possible to allow for fringe.

Handwash in warm water with mild soap.

Lay flat to dry. Make six 2½" (6.5 cm) dense multicolored pom-poms (see page 42).

Attach the pom-poms to the scarf as follows:

Step 1. Divide the warp ends into thirds. Each third will be threaded to one pom-pom so that there are three pom-poms at each end of the scarf.

Divide each third into two groups. Thread one group through a tapestry needle and insert the needle through the middle of the pom-pom.

Step 2. Pull the length through.

Step 3. Thread the other half of the warp yarns in this group through a tapestry needle and insert the needle through the pom-pom right next to the first group of threads.

Step 4. Tightly tie the ends together in a square knot. Hide the knot under the pom-pom pile and trim the ends flush with the edge of the pom-pom.

Step 1

Step 2

Step 3

Step 4

HOW to make a pom-pom with a clover pom-pom maker

You'll need yarn, strong string such as pearl cotton, scissors, and a pom-pom maker to yield a 2½" (6.5 cm) pom-pom. We used a size #45 Clover Pom-pom Maker.

Step 1. Hold the 3 yarns (Fil Royal in gold, Fil Royal in blue, and Timidity) together. Open one side of the pom-pom maker and wrap the 3 yarns together until the side is about half full.

Step 2. Cut off the Timidity and finish winding with the blue and gold Fil Royal until the side is densely full.

Step 3. Wrap the other side as you did for the first side.

Step 4. Close the pom-pom maker and hold securely shut while you insert sharp scissors into the groove and clip the yarn all the way around.

Step 5. Keeping the pom-pom maker closed, insert a strong yarn or string (pearl cotton was used here) in the groove. Cinch tight to secure the cut ends and tie a tight square knot.

Step 6. Pull the sides apart to release the pom-pom and trim any uneveness.

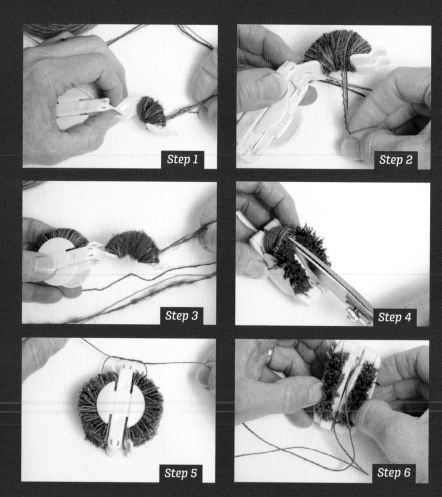

Step 1

Step 2

Step 3

Step 4

Step 5

Step 6

finishing the ends

You always need to finish the ends of a scarf in some way. If the weft is not secured at the ends, your scarf will ravel. The amount that it will ravel depends on the yarn, sett, and finishing. Your options for finishing are hemstitching, knotting, twisting, and fulling. Besides the practical matter of securing the weft, you should choose the finish with the whole design of the scarf in mind. Sometimes, say for a suit jacket, the end finish should be short. Hemstitching would be an appropriate choice. Fringe for a scarf worn with a coat or as an accessory could be longer. You can also get creative with your finishing, making a bold statement as illustrated by our Bobble Scarf. It's playful, bouncing pom-poms punctuate the ends of an otherwise subdued fabric.

2 designing with yarn

Playing around with yarn is a terrific way to create smashingly sumptuous scarves. All of the scarves in this chapter are woven in the simplest structure, plain weave, but nothing is ordinary about this collection when you make yarn the star.

Peruse the selection at your local yarn store to put together yarns that inspire you. Use the guidelines for choosing yarns in this chapter to help you create your own yarn-centric designs.

Choosing a Warp Yarn

For a yarn to be successful in the warp, it needs be strong enough to hold up under tension on the loom. To determine if a yarn will be suitable, hold it between your hands about 4" (10 cm) apart and pull firmly. If the yarn "drifts" when you give it a tug, it won't hold up on the loom. If the yarn breaks with a snap, or you can't break it at all, it's an excellent candidate for a warp.

If your pull-test deems a yarn that you like is too weak for warp, don't worry—you can always use it for weft. The yarn only needs to hold together long enough for you to place it in the shed. That said, if you're dead set on using a weak yarn for warp, minimize potential breakage by pairing it with a strong yarn and weaving under minimal tension.

Considering Yarn Texture

When you evaluate a yarn's suitability for the warp, consider its texture. A fuzzy mohair yarn, with its inviting halo, may catch on its neighbors every time you change the shed, and you may be frustrated by constantly needing to clear the shed of sticking yarns. This is not fun. If you're convinced that you need mohair in the warp, try separating individual mohair warp ends with some type of smooth yarn.

Sett

How you sett a yarn is important for many reasons. First, it's critical to the final hand of the piece. A yarn threaded too closely produces a stiff fabric. Conversely, a yarn threaded too openly results in a floppy fabric. To get an idea of a workable sett, wind the prospective yarn around a ruler for 1" (2.5 cm), placing each wrap right next to its neighbor, never allowing the wraps to overlap. Divide the number of wraps in this inch by two to determine a reasonable number of ends to thread per inch.

When you're determining sett, you'll also want to take into account the fiber content of the yarn. Except for superwash, a wool yarn will bloom more than a linen yarn, which may affect how closely you want to sett the warp. We recommend always weaving a sample before embarking on a project.

It's also important to think about the style of the yarn in your warp. A fuzzy yarn will need more space, as will novelty yarns, such as bouclé, eyelash, and thick-and-thin yarns. Think about threading the textured yarns in the slots (where they'll have more space to move), alternated with smooth yarns threaded in the holes. You might also want to use a wider sett to increase the space between individual warp ends.

Yarn Elasticity

Although you can mix and match yarns of different textures (e.g., crepe, bouclé, eyelash, etc.) and fiber content (e.g., wool, cotton, bamboo, etc.), be aware that dissimilar yarns will behave differently in the warp. Some might stretch more while others may have less give.

When you thread yarns of differing elasticity in broad stripes, tension problems might arise as one section takes up more than the other. This difference causes part of the warp to be very tight and others to be too loose. In extreme cases, some sections might become so tight that the warp ends break. However, if you keep your stripes to ½" (1.3 cm) wide or less, you shouldn't have much problem.

Using Your Stash

You probably have odds and ends of yarn lying about. Although these leftovers may not be enough for an entire project, they can be combined into a smashing woven scarf, such as our Stash Buster Scarf (page 68).

Working from your stash can be a rather organic process, somewhat like designing "on the fly." To begin, choose some likely warp candidates and a reed size appropriate to them (this will help you determine the number of warp ends you'll need).

After you've decided on the warp yarn or yarns, it's time to choose a weft. If you're not sure how much yarn you have in a leftover ball or the yarn is missing a ball band, weigh the yarn, then use a McMorran Yarn Balance (see page 154) to determine if you have enough yards (or meters) for the project you have in mind.

When you make a mixed warp, wind each yarn separately on a warping board (see page 151) until it's gone, or until you have as much as you want. Then thread the heddle from the front, placing yarns helter-skelter across the warp width. If you want the yarns to blend without distinct stripes, don't place any one yarn next to itself in the heddle. Thread fuzzy or fat yarns in the slots, where there will be more room for them to move around. (See our Stash Buster Scarf on page 68 for more detail about mixing yarns.)

Simple Choices

Yarns don't have to be outrageous to make an impact. Simple, beautiful yarns can weave up into the softest and most elegant fabrics. For our Posh Plum Scarf (page 50), for example, we paired a lovely mohair with a smooth linen-blend yarn for a stunning result. While an all-mohair scarf would be soft and have a dreamy drape, it wouldn't have the same visual interest that we got by alternating mohair and linen. Leaving ½" (1.3 cm) sections of mohair in the warp, we contributed to the pleasing overall design. Compare the fabric to the pink variation in which end-on-end stripes are used across the entire warp.

When measuring a warp for end-on-end threading, hold the yarns together to speed the process at the warping board.

Yarn Accents

Sometimes just a little bit of a yarn can make a big impact. For our Ladies Who Lunch Scarf (page 54), we used accents of spaced-dyed eyelash yarn. The windowpane plaid pattern creates bright, crisscrossing lines against a ground of fuzzy mohair. In this case, a little bit of yarn goes a long way.

Unlikely Choices

Some unique yarns are just too interesting to pass by, but once you've bought such a yarn, you may not quite know what to do with it. Our Flower Power Scarf (page 46) might be a case in point. For this scarf, we combined seemingly disparate yarns—both in color and texture—in the warp. We then crossed them with a third highly textured yarn. The result is little textured "flowers" along the length of the scarf.

We encourage you to be bold when you choose your yarns and colors. Create lively warps and experiment with different wefts to come up with your own interesting looks. Have no fear! It's only yarn, after all.

This scarf is really all about the yarn. Three unique, even disparate, yarns are combined to make this unusual piece that's sure to draw comments.

FLOWER POWER

This scarf illustrates the power of choosing a yarn that packs a big punch. Two quite differently textured yarns are alternated in the warp and crossed with a spaced bobble yarn. The thick areas of the weft yarn are lifted to the surface during weaving to form random "flowers." For a reversible, if less dramatic design, you could leave the thick areas of the weft yarn in the shed to produce a thick-and-thin look. At a warp sett of 5 ends per inch, this scarf weaves up in less than two hours— truly a scarf-in-an-afternoon project.

Designed by Stephanie Flynn Sokolov | **Woven by** Betty Paepke

Finished size: 6½" (16.5 cm) wide and 57" (145 cm) long, plus 6" (15 cm) fringe at each end.

Structure: Plain weave.

Equipment: 10" (25.5 cm) wide, 5-dent rigid heddle reed; one stick shuttle.

Yarn: *Trendsetter Bacio* (45% acrylic, 33% wool, 22% nylon at 868 yd/lb [794 m/453 g]) in #908 Foxfire (warp only): 42 yd (1 ball at 95 yd [87 m]/50 g).

Trendsetter Dune (41% mohair, 29% nylon, 30% acrylic at 731 yd/lb [668 m/453 g]) in #113 Country Meadow (warp only): 47 yd (1 ball at 80 yd [73 m]/50 g).

Trendsetter Geisha (64% acrylic, 14% polyamide, 12% wool, 10% polyester at 594 yd/lb [543 m/453 g]) in #5 Navy Blue/Earth (weft only): 80 yd (2 balls at 65 yd [543 m]/453 g).

Warp length: 84" (213 cm), which includes 18" (45.5 cm) for loom waste and 12" (30 cm) for fringe—6" (15 cm) at each end.

Total warp ends: 38.

Width in reed: 7½" (19 cm).

Ends per inch: 5.

Picks per inch: 5.

Yarn Wrapping

This yarn wrapping is shown actual size to assist you in making substitutions. Just place the yarn you want to use on top of the yarn chart to see if the yarn is the same size. Substituting a yarn with similar fiber content will be most successful.

Top to bottom:

➤ Trendsetter Bacio in #908 Foxfire.
➤ Trendsetter Dune in #113 Country Meadow.
➤ Trendsetter Geisha in #5 Navy Blue/ Earth.

Warping

Using the direct peg method (page 146), thread every other slot (thread a slot, skip a slot) with Dune, measuring a total of 20 ends (10 slots). Then thread the Bacio, filling in the slots not threaded with Dune, according to the warping plan below.

Warping Plan

	Repeat 9 times		End	
Dune	2		2	20
Bacio		2		18
Total Ends				**38**

Weaving

Wind Geisha on the stick shuttle.

Allow sufficient length in your front tie-on for a 6" (15 cm) fringe.

Use a light hand and beat at 5 ppi for a balanced weave. Resist over-beating and making the fabric too stiff.

To create the "flowers," lift the textured lumps up out of the shed between 2 warp threads before beating, as shown at right. To ensure the flowers are secured between the warp threads, lay the weft in at a very small angle.

As you beat, pull the "flowers" up between the warps where they naturally fall.

If the "flowers" bunch too closely in a small area, cut off the weft yarn to eliminate a flower and reinsert the yarn in the shed, placing the next flower in a different location.

Weave as far as the warp length allows, about 66" (167 cm).

▲ *Step 1. Place the yarn in the shed at a shallow angle.*

Finishing

Remove the fabric from the loom, untying the knots in front to allow for fringe.

Tie groups of 4 warp ends each into overhand knots (see page 57) close to the edge of the fabric. Handwash in very warm water with gentle agitation. Lay flat to dry. Lightly steam-press on the wrong side as needed with a pressing cloth.

▲ *Step 2. Lift the "flowers" out of the shed, bringing them to the surface. If the flower seems to hang out too far, draw part of it into the shed to snug it up a bit.*

Variation

➤ This narrow version is woven in the same yarns but in a different colorway. The colors are Bacio in #328 French Vanilla, Dune in #88 Rust, Navy, Plum-Multi, and Geisha in #9 Charcoal Multi.

Woven by
Stephanie Flynn Sokolov

▲ *Step 3. Gently beat the weft into place.*

Beautiful, elegant yarns weave up easily for this lovely airy scarf that's light as a feather. This design would also translate well for a shawl woven on a wider loom.

POSH PLUM

Mixing yarns doesn't have to be complicated. For this scarf, we alternated two yarns in the warp: a fine mohair and a blend of wool, linen, and alpaca. The mohair yarn is threaded in the slots to allow extra space for it to move around in the reed. Additional textural interest is created by warping narrow ½" (1.3 cm) stripes of just mohair at regular intervals. A light hand is used to beat the mohair weft to produce a scarf with lots of drape.

Designed by Stephanie Flynn Sokolov and Jane Patrick | **Woven by** Betty Paepke

Finished size: 7½" (19 cm) wide and 75" (190.5 cm) long, plus 6" (15 cm) fringe at each end.

Structure: Plain weave.

Equipment: 10" (25.5 cm) wide, 8-dent rigid heddle reed; one stick shuttle; tapestry needle.

Yarn: *Classic Elite Pirouette* (67% kid mohair, 25% bamboo viscose, 8% nylon at 4,475 yd/lb [3,092 m/453 g]) in Dried Lavender (warp and weft): 360 yd (2 balls at 246 yd [224 m]/25 g).

Classic Elite Soft Linen (35% wool, 35% linen, 30% baby alpaca at 1,245 yd lb [1,138 m/453 g]) in Lavender (warp only): 70 yd (1 ball at 137 yd [125 m]/50 g).

Warp length: 96" (244 cm), which includes 18" (45.5 cm) for loom waste and 12" (30 cm) for fringe—6" (15 cm) at each end.

Total warp ends: 71.

Width in reed: 8¾" (22 cm).

Ends per inch: 8.

Picks per inch: 10.

Yarn Wrapping

This yarn wrapping is shown actual size to assist you in making substitutions. Just place the yarn you want to use on top of the yarn chart to see if the yarn is the same size. Substituting a yarn with similar fiber content will be most successful.

Top to bottom:

➤ Classic Elite Pirouette in Dried Lavender.

➤ Classic Elite Soft Linen in Lavender.

Warping

Use the indirect method to measure the warp on a warping board (see page 151), following the warping plan below. When threading, begin in a slot and end in a slot.

Warping Plan

| | | Repeat 4 times | | | | |
		5 times		5 times		
Pirouette	3	1	4	1	2	46
Soft Linen		1		1		25
Total Ends						71

Weaving

Wind Pirouette on the stick shuttle.

Allow sufficient length in your front tie-on for a 6" (15 cm) fringe.

Leaving a tail four times the weaving width for hemstitching, weave 3 picks, then beat tightly to compact them together.

Use the tail to hemstitch (see page 153) over 4 warp ends and 3 weft picks.

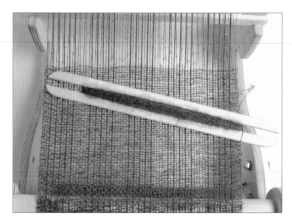

▲ *The weave is quite open, as shown in this in-process photo.*

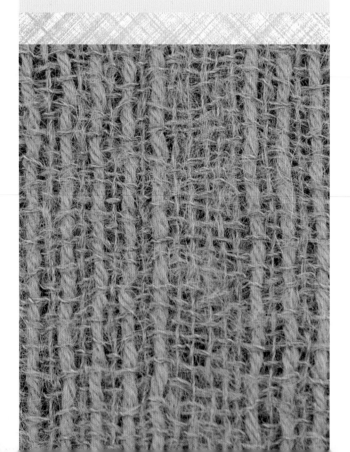

Weave at 10 ppi using a light beat—almost as if you're gently pushing the yarns into place—until scarf measures 78" (198 cm).

Hemstitch over 4 warps and 3 wefts.

Remove the fabric from the loom, untying knots in the front to allow for fringe.

Finishing

Handwash in very warm water with gentle agitation.

Roll the scarf in a towel to remove excess moisture.

Place the scarf and a towel in the dryer on the low setting for about 20 minutes or until dry, checking often to monitor the fulling process and removing the scarf when the desired hand is achieved.

Steam-press using a pressing cloth.

Trim fringe using a ruler, rotary cutter, and healing mat.

Variation

➤ The same yarns are used in this rose variation. One end each of Pirouette (#4088 Electric Salmon) and Soft Linen (#2288 Tea Rose) alternate across the entire warp.

Designed by Stephanie Flynn Sokolov

Here, a little bit of a contrasting yarn goes a long way to create a unique look. The accent yarn is a variegated spaced eyelash yarn that creates little dots of color when woven. The trick to creating the look is alternating an end of the eyelash yarn with an end of the mohair so that each eyelash yarn is given enough space to speak for itself.

LADIES WHO LUNCH

Two novelty yarns—one a fuzzy mohair and the other a variegated spaced eyelash—produce an enchanting mix of color and texture. The scarf looks sophisticated, but is so simple to execute. The two yarns are woven as they are threaded in the warp for a balanced windowpane plaid. Impossibly soft and light, this scarf weaves up quickly, and the open weave structure shows off the lovely way that kid mohair blooms in the finishing process.

Designed and woven by Cei Lambert

Finished size: 7¾" (19.5 cm) wide and 76" (193 cm) long, plus 4" (10 cm) fringe at each end.

Structure: Plain weave.

Equipment: 10" (25.5 cm) wide, 8-dent rigid heddle reed; two stick shuttles.

Yarn: *Mango Moon Capra* (70% mohair, 30% silk at 4,909 yd lb [4,488 m/453 g]) in Cocoa (warp and weft): 300 yd (2 skeins at 270 yd [246 m]/25 g).

Mango Moon Parade (100% rayon variegated spaced eyelash at 2,727 yd/lb [2,493 m/453 g]) in Earth (warp and weft): 70 yd (1 skein at 150 yd [137 m]/25 g).

Warp length: 100" (254 cm), which allows 20" (51 cm) for loom waste and includes 8" (20 cm) for fringe—4" (10 cm) at each end.

Total warp ends: 64.

Width in reed: 8" (20.5 cm).

Ends per inch: 8.

Picks per inch: 8.

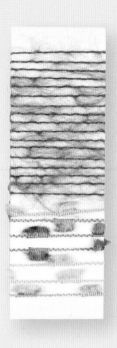

Yarn Wrapping

This yarn wrapping is shown actual size to assist you in making substitutions. Just place the yarn you want to use on top of the yarn chart to see if the yarn is the same size. Substituting a yarn with similar fiber content will be most successful.

Top to bottom:

➤ Mango Moon Capra in Cocoa.
➤ Mango Moon Parade in Earth.

Warping

Use the indirect method to measure the warp on a warping board (see page 151), following the warping plan on page 59.

Weaving

Wind Capra and Parade on separate shuttles.

Leave at least 4" (10 cm) of space from the apron rod to allow for fringe.

Weave at 8 ppi in balanced plain weave in the same pattern used to warp the loom as follows:

14 picks of Capra, 1 pick of Parade, 1 pick of Capra, 1 pick of Parade, 1 pick of Capra, 1 pick of Parade (3 picks of Parade total).

Repeat this sequence for the length of the scarf, ending with 14 picks of Capra.

Notes: *Selvedges are an important consideration with this piece because the Capra yarn is apt to fly away while you weave. For best results, don't pull the selvedges too tightly and do adjust the yarn at the selvedge as necessary, even after a pick has been pressed into place.*

Because Capra contains kid mohair, it's quite fuzzy and can stick to itself or create little fuzz balls. If any stickiness occurs, gently maneuver the yarns with your fingers until the pick can be beaten into place easily. If a fuzz ball begins to develop, carefully pick it out with your fingernails or tweezers. The small difficulties the fuzziness can cause are rewarded in the amazingly soft hand of the finished fabric!

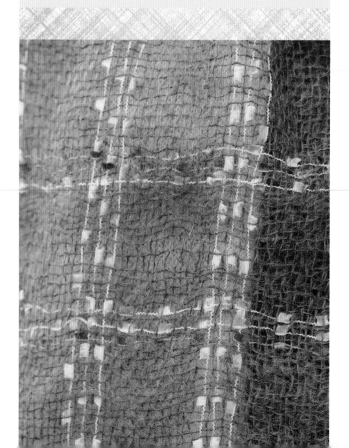

Tying a Knotted Fringe

An easy way to finish the ends of a scarf is by knotting groups of warp threads to prevent the weft from raveling. Do this before washing, but don't trim the ends until after the scarf has been washed.

Step 1. Place a weight on top of the edge of the scarf to keep the scarf in place. Working along the edge of a table will help tie knots evenly along the edge. For this example, we used three warp ends per group. Take the leftmost warp end of this group and place it in the next group to the left, then take the rightmost warp end from the next group and place it into this first group—the cross between groups holds the last weft pick in place, preventing it from floating down between the two knots.

Step 2. Make a loose overhand knot.

Step 3. Gently slide the knot to the edge of the weaving before tightening.

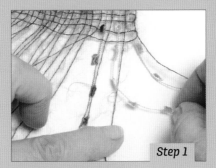
Step 1

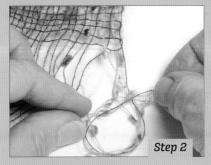
Step 2

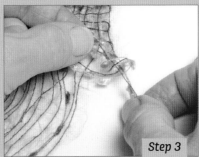
Step 3

Finishing

Remove the fabric from the loom, untying the knots in front to allow for fringe.

Working in groups of 3 warp ends each, work a knotted fringe (see page 57) across each end.

Handwash in very hot water (use rubber gloves if necessary) with mild detergent.

Rinse in very hot water, then gently squeeze out moisture and lay flat to dry.

If pressing is needed, use a medium setting and a damp pressing cloth.

Trim the fringe with a rotary cutter against a straight edge on a healing mat.

▲ *For each 3-row sequence of Parade, begin and end the yarn by weaving the tail into the shed for about ½" (1.3 cm). Leave the end hanging out and trim it flush with the surface of the weaving only after the scarf has been washed and pressed.*

Warping Plan

		Repeat 3 times							
Capra, Cocoa	1	1	1	14		1	1	1	52
Parade, Earth		1	1	1	1		1	1	12
	Total Ends								**64**

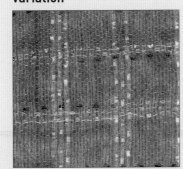

Variation

➤ Here is the very same project in a different colorway. We used Mango Moon Capra in Heron and Parade in Lunar.

Designed by Cei Lambert

By skipping pairs of slots and holes (see the Warping Plan), the warp yarns are allowed to breathe and contribute to the soft drape of the finished scarf. Additionally, variable beating of the weft is important. The finer weft is packed in at 12 ppi and the fuzzy mohair at 6.

MIDNIGHT IN PARIS

Three yarns are combined in this highly textured, luxurious scarf—a fine laceweight tussah silk/merino wool frames a fuzzy mohair, and a cotton tape with multicolored slub accents dances along the length of the scarf. This fabric will be quite open on the loom as you weave, especially in the warp and weft stripes of the Blackberry wool/silk. Don't worry—you'll heavily full these areas during the finishing process to create the windowpane effect.

Designed and woven by Stephanie Flynn Sokolov

Finished size: 9" (23 cm) wide and 60" (152.5 cm) long, plus 6" (15 cm) fringe at each end.

Structure: Plain weave.

Equipment: 15" (38 cm) wide, 12-dent rigid heddle reed; two stick shuttles; rubber gloves.

Yarn: *Lorna's Laces Helen's Lace* (50% tussah silk, 50% merino wool at 5,000 yd/lb [4,572 m/453 g]) in Blackberry (warp and weft): 185 yd (1 skein at [1, 250 yd [1,143 m]/4 oz).

Lorna's Laces Glory (mohair/wool blend at 1,097 yd/lb [1,003 m/453 g]) in Navy (warp and weft): 240 yd (2 skeins at [120 yd [109 m]/1.75 oz).

Skacel Tamarillo (100% cotton tape with multicolor slubs at 1,298 yd/lb [1,186 m/453 g] in #43 Dark Blue (warp only): 45 yd (1 ball at 142 yd [129 m]/50 g).

Warp length: 93" (236 cm), which allows 24" (61 cm) for loom waste and includes 12" (30.5 cm) for fringe—6" (15 cm) at each end.

Total warp ends: 88.

Width in reed: 12½" (31.5 cm).

Ends per inch: About 7.

Picks per inch: 12 for Helen's Laces; 6 for Glory.

Yarn Wrapping

This yarn wrapping is shown actual size to assist you in making substitutions. Just place the yarn you want to use on top of the yarn chart to see if the yarn is the same size. Substituting a yarn with similar fiber content will be most successful.

Top to bottom:

➤ Lorna's Laces Helen's Lace in Blackberry.

➤ Lorna's Laces Glory in Navy.

➤ Skacel Tamarillo in #43 Dark Blue.

Warping

Use the indirect method to measure each yarn on the warping board (see page 151) as follows: 40 ends of Helen's Laces, 32 ends of Glory, and 16 ends of Tamarillo.

Thread the heddle following the warping plan below.

Warping Plan

		Repeat 8 times							
Helen's Laces	2*	4						6	40
Glory			2			2			32
Tamarillo					2				16
Skip**			2	2		2	2		
Total Ends									88

*begin in a slot **a total of 64 spaces are skipped.*

Weaving

Wind Helen's Lace and Glory on separate stick shuttles.

Allow sufficient length in your front tie-on for a 6" (10 cm) fringe. Leaving a tail four times the weaving width for hemstitching, weave 9 picks with Helen's Lace.

Use the tail to hemstitch (see page 153) over 3 warp ends and 3 weft picks.

Weave 12 picks of Glory at 6 ppi (about 2" [5 cm]).

Weave 6 picks of Helen's Lace at 12 ppi (about ½" [1.3 cm]).

Repeat these 18 picks until a total of 69" (175 cm) have been woven, ending with 12 picks of Helen's Lace.

Hemstitch with Helen's Lace over 3 warps and 3 wefts.

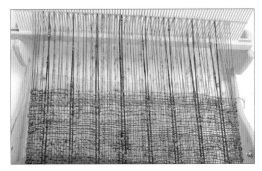

▲ *The fabric on the loom is woven quite open. Use a light touch to beat.*

▲ *The woven fabric before finishing.*

Finishing

Untie the warp from the apron rods and remove from the loom. Your scarf will be quite open. The finishing process is critical to producing the final beautiful result.

Place the scarf in hot water and let it soak for 10 minutes.

Add a small amount of liquid soap, then gently rub the Helen's Lace yarn in both directions along the warp and the weft (use rubber gloves) while trying your best not to agitate the mohair.

Place in the dryer under the no-heat setting for 10 minutes.

Hang or lay flat until completely dry.

Steam-press using a press cloth.

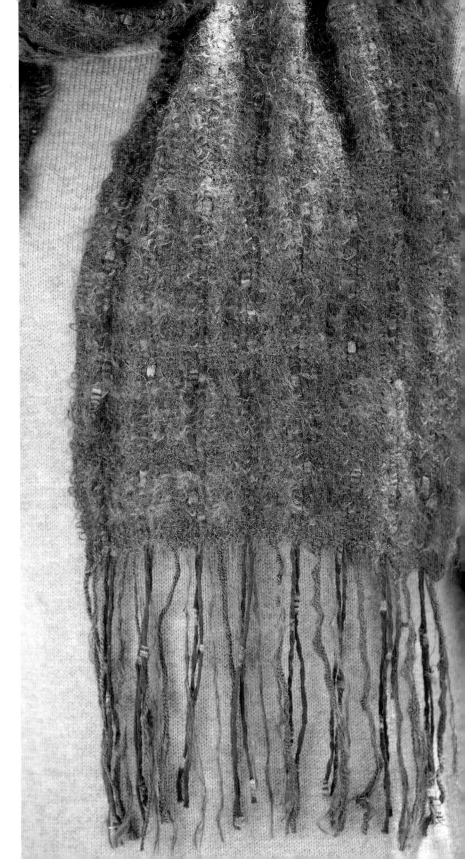

The fabric is merely plain weave, but when it's scrunched and layered around the neck, a sophisticated edgy look is achieved. Although you might think that the stainless steel would make a harsh surface, the silk surrounding it is soft, producing a yarn—and fabric—that is artistic and wearable.

STAINLESS STEEL SCARF

If you were told that someone had woven a most wearable scarf out of stainless steel, would you believe it? As improbable as it seems, this open-weave scarf is woven with just that. The laceweight yarn used here has a stainless steel core wrapped with silk. On the cone, it looks like an ordinary laceweight yarn, but it weaves into a fabric that can be squished and willhold its shape.

Designed and woven by Stephanie Flynn Sokolov

Finished size: 8½" (21.5 cm) wide and 84" (213 cm) long, plus 5" (12.5 cm) fringe at each end.

Structure: Plain weave.

Equipment: 10" (25.5 cm) wide, 12-dent rigid heddle reed; one stick shuttle; tapestry needle; thick paper to roll between layers on the cloth beam; rotary cutter and healing mat for trimming fringe.

Yarn: *Habu A-20 Silk Stainless Steel* (69% silk, 31% stainless steel at 9,952 yd/lb [9,100 m/453 g]) in #1 Off White (warp and weft):

360 yd (329 m) for warp and 260 yd (237 m) for weft (2 cones at 311 yd [277 m]/0.5 oz).

Warp length: 108" (274 cm), which allows 24" (61 cm) for loom waste and includes 10" (25 cm) for fringe—5" (12.5 cm) at each end.

Total warp ends: 120.

Width in reed: 10" (25.5 cm).

Ends per inch: 12.

Picks per inch: 10.

Yarn Wrapping

This yarn wrapping is shown actual size to assist you in making substitutions. Just place the yarn you want to use on top of the yarn chart to see if the yarn is the same size. Substituting a yarn with similar fiber content will be most successful.

➤ Habu A-20 Silk Stainless Steel in #1 Off White.

Warping

Use the direct peg method (page 146) to thread the reed.

Weaving

Wind Silk Stainless Steel on the stick shuttle.

Allow sufficient length in your front tie-on for a 5" (12.5 cm) fringe. Leaving a tail four times the weaving width for hemstitching, weave 3 picks and beat firmly to compact them together.

Use the tail to hemstitch (see page 153) over 1 warp end and 3 weft picks.

To keep the selvedges straight and the weft evenly spaced, beat after every 3 picks and hold the weft taut while beating.

Weave at 10 ppi until piece measures 84" (213 cm).

Hemstitch over 1 warp and 3 wefts.

Note: *The beauty of this scarf is in the yarn, but because this yarn doesn't stretch and is "wiry," it requires special handling. Crank up the tension on the loom as much as possible and use a light hand while beating so that the weft doesn't pack in too closely to the previous pick. Place thick paper between layers as you roll the weaving onto the cloth beam to help maintain even tension as you weave.*

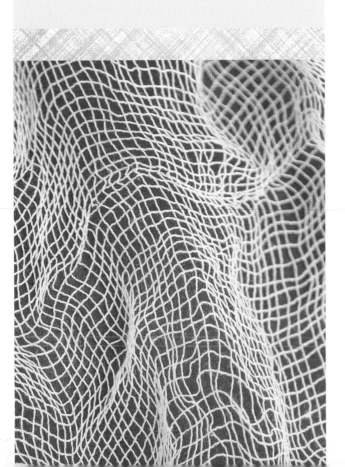

▲ *The scarf, shown removed from loom, is open and airy.*

Finishing

Remove the fabric from the loom, untying the knots in front to allow for the fringe.

Lay the scarf on a healing mat on a flat surface and use a rotary cutter and ruler to cut the fringe to 5" (12.5 cm) at each end.

We did not wet-finish this scarf—dry cleaning is recommended.

Scrunch the fabric as you like.

A variety of yarn styles and fiber content make up our fringy Stash Buster Scarf. We've given the actual yarns used for this scarf, but we encourage you to mix and match yarns from your own stash. Quite small amounts are required of each warp yarn; in some cases, just a few yards. So we encourage you to dive into your yarn basket to choose yarns for this piece.

STASH BUSTER

Everyone who works with yarn has some sort of private stash. And everyone wonders what to do with it. It seems criminal to throw away perfectly good yarn; on the other hand, what do you do with all those dibby-dabs? Enter our Stash Buster Scarf. In stash-busting, weaving has an advantage over knitting—you can use bits and pieces of this and that to create remarkable and quick results. If you're unsure of how much yarn you have, a yarn balance (see page 155) will provide the answer.

Designed and woven by Stephanie Flynn Sokolov

Finished size: 3¼" (8.5 cm) wide and 58" (147.5 cm) long, plus 3" (7.5 cm) of fringe on all four sides.

Structure: Plain weave with weft fringe.

Equipment: 10" (25.5 cm) wide, 8-dent rigid heddle reed; one stick shuttle; crochet hook.

Yarn: Because we've used many yarns in the warp, we've numbered them. These numbers correspond to the warping plan and will make substitutions easier.

1. Webs 20/2 Silk (100% silk at 5,400 yd/lb [4,937 m/453 g]) in Orange: 20 yd (warp only).

2. Jaggerspun 2/18 Superfine Merino (100% merino wool at 5,040 yd/lb [4,608 m/453 g]) in Burnt Orange (warp only): 58 yd.

3. S Charles Crystal (85% polyester/15% cotton at 2,618 yd/lb [5,411 m/453 g]) in #10 Sunset (warp only): 10 yd.

4. Brown Sheep Cotton Fleece (80% cotton, 20% wool at 982 yd/lb [897 m/g]) in #CW-310 Wild Orange (warp only): 20 yd.

5. Orlon Nylon Bouclé (Orlon/nylon blend at 2,700 yd lb [2,468 m/453 g]) in Pimento (warp only): 10 yd. *Note: This is a mill-end yarn.*

6. S. Charles Eclipse (92% cotton, 4% polyester, 4% nylon at 1,481 yd/lb [1,354 m/453 g]) in #04 Coral (warp only): 5 yd.

7. Erdal Eyelash Tweed (100% polyester at 364 yd/lb [333 m/453 g]) in #38 Orange (warp only): 2.5 yd.

8. Brown Sheep Lamb's Pride Bulky (85% wool, 15% mohair at 500 yd/lb [457 m/453 g]) in #M235 Wine Splash (weft only): 75 yd for weft plus 8 yd for end fringe (1 skein at 125 yd [114 m]/4 oz).

9. Be Sweet Bamboo (100% bamboo at 1,005 yd/lb [918 m/kg]) in #671 Garnet (weft only): 70 yd (1 ball at 110 yd [100 m]/100 g).

Warp length: 85" (216 cm), which allows 24" (61 cm) for loom waste and includes 6" (15 cm) for fringe—3" (7.5 cm) at each end.

Total warp ends: 43 working ends (actual number of ends varies due to some used doubled).

Width in reed: Just over 5" (12.5 cm).

Ends per inch: 8 (working ends).

Picks per inch: 8.

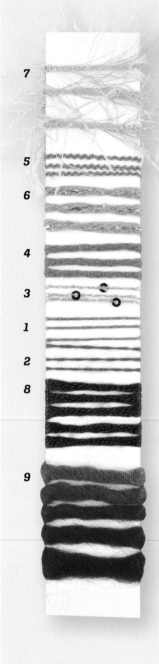

Yarn Wrapping

This yarn wrapping is shown actual size to assist you in making substitutions. Just place the yarn you want to use on top of the yarn chart to see if the yarn is the same size. Substituting a yarn with similar fiber content will be most successful.

Top to bottom:

➤ **7.** Erdal Eyelash Tweed in #38 Orange.

➤ **5.** Orlon Nylon Bouclé in Pimento.

➤ **6.** S. Charles Eclipse in #04 Coral.

➤ **4.** Brown Sheep Cotton Fleece in #CW-310 Wild Orange.

➤ **3.** S Charles Crystal in Sunset.

➤ **1.** Webs 20/2 Silk in Orange.

➤ **2.** Jaggerspun 2/18 Superfine Merino in Burnt Orange.

➤ **8.** Be Sweet Bamboo in #671 Garnet (weft).

➤ **9.** Brown Sheep Lamb's Pride Bulky in Wine Splash (weft).

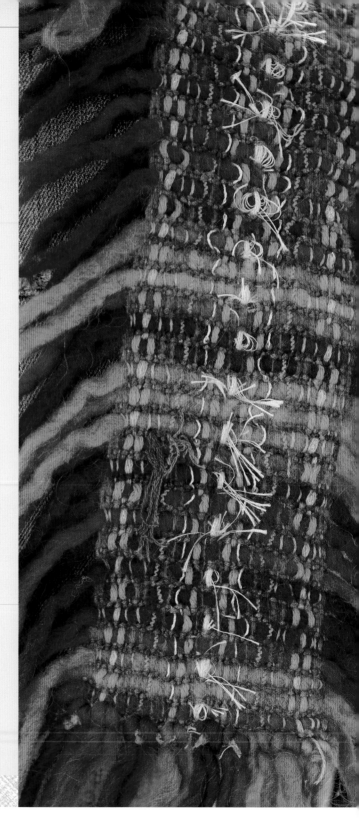

Warping

Use the indirect method to measure the yarns separately on the warping board (see page 151), following the warping plan below.

Weaving

Wind Be Sweet Bamboo on the stick shuttle.

Allow sufficient length in your front tie-on for a 3" (7.5 cm) fringe. Leaving a tail about four times the width of the weaving for hemstitching, weave 3 picks of bamboo.

Use the tail to hemstitch (see page 153) over 2 warp ends and 2 weft picks.

Draw out a length of Brown Sheep Bulky right from the ball and insert it in the shed, allowing between 3" and 3½" (7.5 and 9 cm) to hang out from each edge. Cut the yarn. Beat.

Carry the bamboo yarn up the selvedge, placing it over or under the bulky yarn to secure it in place and weave 2 more picks of bamboo yarn.

Repeat by placing the bulky yarn in the next shed, trim, beat, then weave 2 picks of bamboo,

changing the shed and beating after each pick. Alternately weave the bamboo weft over or under the bulky weft along the selvedges to make tidy edges.

Continue weaving in this manner until you can't weave any further.

Hemstitch with bamboo over 2 warps and 2 wefts.

▲ Insert the bulky yarn into the shed directly from the ball, leaving about 3" to 3½" (7.5 to 9 cm) hanging at each edge. Eyeball the lengths and vary them somewhat for a ragged edge.

Warping Plan

Yarn																	
1		1		1			1		1								8
2	2x		2x				2x		2x		1	1			1	1*	23
3													1	1			4
4				1		1									1	1	8
5								1	1								4
6					1												2
7																1	1
Total Actual Ends																**51****	

1. *Webs 20/2 Silk*

2. *Jaggerspun*

3. *S Charles Crystal*

4. *Brown Sheep Cotton Fleece*

5. *Orlon Nylon*

6. *S. Charles Eclipse*

7. *Erdal Eyelash Tweed*

2x = a yarn doubled in that position in the reed
*Reverse from this point
**Total number of ends: 51 (43 working ends)

Finishing

Remove the fabric from the loom, untying the knots in front to allow for fringe.

Tie the warp fringe into overhand knots, then trim the yarns close to the knots.

Cut eighteen 16" (40.5 cm) lengths of bulky weft for additional fringe at each short end. To attach the fringe, fold a length in half and use a crochet hook to pull the loop through the end of the scarf, as shown at right. Slip the 2 ends through the loop and pull snug to secure, hiding the close-cropped knots. Attach nine fringes to each short end.

Handwash in very warm water.

Place the scarf and a towel in the dryer on the low setting until dry, checking often to ensure against over-fulling.

Steam-press with a pressing cloth, smoothing out the fringe to tame it.

Variation

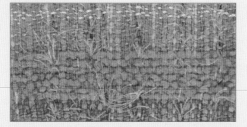

➤ We put together all of our orange yarns to create this highly textured variation. We used a variety of textures and yarn weights in the warp and sett at 5 epi. The weft stripes reuse some of the warp yarns, but other yarns are incorporated as well. Different sizes of weft stripes contribute to the cacophony of texture that's pure pleasure to weave.

Designed by Jane Patrick and Cei Lambert

Applying Fringe

▲ *Trim the warp close to the overhand knots, then use a crochet hook to pull the loop through the end of scarf.*

▲ *Slip the 2 loose ends through the loop to secure it in place.*

tips for combining yarns

➤ When you choose colors from your stash, pool the colors that interest you and make a wrapping of what you might want your warp to look like. Monochromatic color schemes are pleasing to the eye and easy to sample. Keep all the colors cool or all the colors warm to simplify the design process and create a successful springboard for stash-busting.

➤ In combining many different types of yarns, you'll most likely need to accommodate a variety of yarn weights. For this scarf, we've doubled some of the finer yarns but left the heavier yarns in a slot or hole of their own. Evening out the yarn sizes in this way ensures that the woven fabric will be relatively balanced.

➤ It's also helpful to consider the fiber content of the yarn you choose. For example, if you want your weaving to have a uniform surface, you'll be more apt to achieve this result if you use yarns with similar fiber content. Mixing fiber contents of yarns that will shrink with those that won't will give your surface more irregularity. On the other hand, alternating shrinking yarns with nonshrinking yarns end by end equalizes their effects, resulting in a smoother finished surface. Because many surprises come from combining yarns, we encourage you to weave a sample before you dive into a project.

➤ Always use a pressing cloth when you use novelty yarns—you don't want to singe your eyelashes!

3 exploring pattern

Up until now, all of the scarves have been woven in plain weave—over, under, over, under. But plenty of other patterns and textures can be woven on the rigid heddle loom to give your scarves a different look and feel. You have two general options when it comes to woven textures—patterns made with a pick-up stick or finger-controlled patterns in which the warp ends or weft picks are manipulated by hand.

Pick-Up

To understand how pick-up works on the rigid heddle loom, look at the warp ends when the heddle rests in the neutral position. Notice how the ends in the holes are fixed whereas those in the slots are free to move up and down. Think of these slot ends as your magic threads. Because they can move in the slots, they're easily manipulated. Your magic wand, so to speak, is your pick-up stick—a flat, smooth stick with at least one pointy end and at least as long as the warp is wide. You'll use the pick-up stick to create another shed (or sheds). In other words, it creates different combinations of lifted and lowered threads. The result is that selected warp ends or selected parts of weft picks float over adjacent ones in an interlacement that interrupts the over-under-over-under structure of plain weave.

To prepare your warp ends for pick-up, place the heddle in the down position so that the slot ends (the "magic" ones) are raised. Working behind the heddle, use the pointy end of your pick-up stick to "pick up" selected raised ends by dipping the stick up and down along these raised warps. For this example, let's pick up every other raised warp. When you get to the edge of the warp, slide the pick-up stick to the back of the loom until it is needed.

The way you use the pick-up stick depends on whether you want to weave warp or weft floats; you can make both with the same pick-up stick. For weft floats, place the heddle in the neutral (neither up nor down) position. Bring the pick-up stick forward, then turn it on edge to create a shed. For warp floats, place the heddle in the up position and slide the pick-up stick forward to the heddle without turning it on edge. Doing so causes warp ends from the bottom of the shed to come to the surface. These two pick-up sheds are used in combination with the up-and-down plain-weave positions to create a variety of float patterns.

Weaving Weft Floats

Step 1. Put the heddle in the down position so that the slot ends are on the top. If you pick-up the holes, you'll find that you can't make a shed with your pick-up stick.

Step 2. To make it easier to see the raised threads, temporarily insert a sheet of paper into the shed. Using the pointy end, use your pick-up stick to pick up the already raised warp ends according to the pattern. In this case, alternate picking 1 up, 1 down.

Step 3. After you pick up all of the threads, slide the pick-up stick to the back of the loom and return the heddle to the neutral position.

Step 4. With the heddle in neutral, bring the pick-up stick up to just behind the heddle and turn it on edge to create weft floats. In this case, the weft goes over 3 warp ends and under 1 to create longer weft floats on the surface.

▶ To raise the slot threads, place the heddle in the down position.

Step 1

◀ On the raised threads only, pick 1 up, 1 down across the entire warp.

Step 2

▶ Store the pick-up stick at the back of the loom until you need it.

Step 3

◀ Create weft floats by placing the heddle in neutral and turn the pick-up stick on edge.

Step 4a

▶ The weft goes over 3 warp threads and under 1 to create longer weft floats on the surface of the fabric.

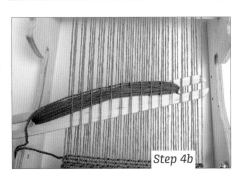

Step 4b

Weaving Warp Floats

Without changing the pick-up stick used for the weft floats, you can make warp floats by simply using the pick-up stick differently. Instead of placing the heddle in neutral, put it in the up position so that the holes are raised. Leaving the pick-up stick flat (don't turn it on edge), slide it up to behind the heddle. Doing so draws up the warp (slot) ends from the bottom of the shed to the top.

Try this pattern:

Step 1. Place the heddle in the down position and weave across.

Step 2. Place the heddle in the up position, slide the pick-up stick up behind it, and weave across.

Step 3. Place the heddle in the down position and weave across.

Step 4. Place the heddle in the up position and weave across.

Repeat Steps 1–4 until you see a pattern develop.

There are scores of patterns you can create with pick-up sticks. If you want to explore more possibilities, check out Jane's *A Weaver's Idea Book*, which covers pick-up patterns in depth.

Note: *To make it easy to see what's going on when you pick up warp ends, you can pick them up in front of the heddle, then transfer them to a pick-up stick behind the heddle. If you have trouble distinguishing between the upper and lower warp ends, place a strip of paper into the shed to hide the lower ends.*

► *To weave warp floats, place the heddle in the up position and leaving the pick-up flat, slide it up to behind the heddle.*

Finger-Controlled Weaves

Finger-controlled weaves are exactly that—weaves (or textures) that are created by hand. Finger-controlled techniques can be grouped into two categories: those that make holes and those that create a three-dimensional (or pile) surface. Finger-controlled weaves are readily accessible—they can be used at any time, anywhere in any fabric. They're infinitely versatile and have oodles of variations. Perhaps the only drawback to finger-controlled techniques is the time required to execute them. They do involve a bit of fiddling around. However, what you spend in time, you gain in novelty—truly smashing results that no machine could ever make. Now that's a true handwoven!

Leno

Leno is a particular structure made by twisting warp ends around one another; the twists are held in place by the following weft pick. Leno is particularly useful as a lace weave because it creates holes in the cloth where the warp ends twist. A wonderful advantage is that the twists are stable, which makes leno a great choice when you want a very open, yet durable, weave. The twisted ends are locked in place and create lasting spaces in the woven web. The basic technique for working leno on a closed shed is shown here. You'll find a fascinating variation in our Lattice Scarf (page 98).

Weaving 2:2 Leno on a Closed Shed

In this version of leno, the heddle is placed in neutral (neither up nor down) and 2 warp ends are twisted over another 2 warp ends. This version is designated 2:2 leno. You can also make different groupings, such as 1:1, 3:3, and odd numbers such as 1:3. As with pick-up patterns, leno offers you endless variations.

To begin, place the heddle in neutral.

Step 1. Working right to left, place warp ends 3 and 4 over ends 1 and 2.

Step 2. Bring warp ends 1 and 2 up to the top and place on a pick-up stick or your finger. Move onto the next 4 warp ends, placing 7 and 8 over 5 and 6. Continue across the warp in this manner until you reach the opposite selvedge.

Step 3. After you create twists all the way across the warp, turn the pick-up stick on edge and insert the shuttle through the shed to lock the twist in place.

Step 4. Press the weft in place by sliding the pick-up stick forward.

Step 5. Open the shed (by putting the heddle either up or down) and weave plain weave back across to the other selvedge so the warps return to their original position.

Step 6. Beat the weft so that the spaces above and below the leno twists are equal.

Repeat Steps 1–6 for another row of leno.

▶ Place warp ends 3 and 4 over ends 1 and 2.

Step 1

◀ Hold the twist on your finger or a pick-up stick.

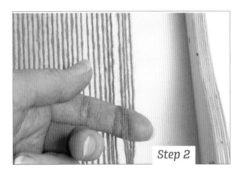

Step 2

▶ Turn the pick-up stick on edge and insert the shuttle.

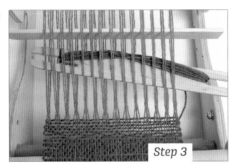

Step 3

◀ Slide the pick-up stick forward.

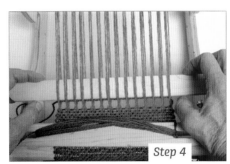

Step 4

▶ Weave back across in a plain-weave shed.

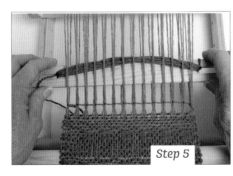

Step 5

◀ Beat the weft so the spaces are even.

Step 6

exploring pattern

Spanish Lace

If you weave back and forth in one section, then back and forth in another section, and so on, you can weave Spanish lace to create holes or patterns in your fabric. Depending on the yarns you use and the number of weft passes in each section, you can create patterns that range from subtle to dramatic. For our Eyelet Scarf (page 92), we made large holes just by weaving many weft rows in each section, then pulling the weft tight to exaggerate the holes.

Weaving Spanish Lace

Step 1. Beginning at the right for the first pick, open the shed (heddle up) and place the shuttle into the shed.

Step 2. Count over 5 raised warp ends, then bring the shuttle out of the shed. Beat lightly.

Step 3. Change sheds for the second pick and weave back to the right selvedge, traveling under 5 raised warp ends. Beat lightly.

Step 4. Repeat Steps 1–3 for as many rows as desired. In this example, one more repeat is worked.

Step 5. To move to the next section, open the shed and weave across the first section (5 raised warp ends) and across the next section (5 more raised warp ends), for a total of 10 raised warp ends. Weave back and forth across this section as you did in the first.

▶ Beginning at the right edge, place the shuttle in the shed.

Step 1

◀ Bring the shuttle out of the shed after 5 raised warp ends. Beat.

Step 2

▶ Change sheds and weave back to the right selvedge. Beat.

Step 3

◀ Weave the third pick the same as the first. Beat.

Step 4a

Step 6. Repeat Steps 1–5, working your way across the warp, using a hand beater or fork to press the weft into place for each section.

Step 7. When you reach the other edge, change sheds and continue in plain weave.

Helpful Hints

► Always count raised warp threads.
► Groups never share warp threads.
► Change sheds for each pass of the shuttle.

► *Beat the weft into place after each row.*

Step 4b

◄ *Weave the fourth pick the same as the second. Beat.*

Step 4c

► *Weave under 10 raised ends to weave the next section.*

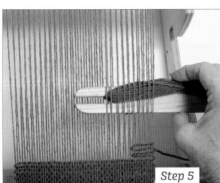

Step 5

◄ *Use a hand beater to beat the subsequent sections into place.*

Step 6a

► *Weave back and forth as you did for the first section.*

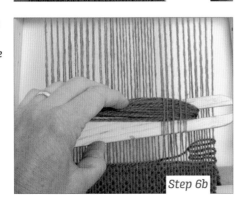

Step 6b

◄ *Change sheds when you reach the other edge and weave across to the right selvedge.*

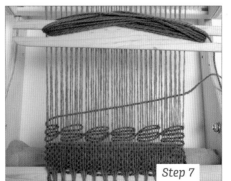

Step 7

► *Insert cut lengths under 2 warp ends.*

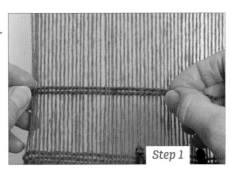

Step 1

► *Bring the ends together, then use your fingers to open the space between the 2 warp ends.*

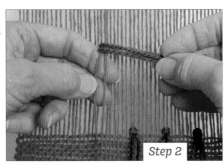

Step 2

► *Bring the ends up through the center and pull to tighten.*

Step 3

► *Weave at least 2 picks of plain weave to secure.*

Step 4

Ghiordes Knots

Ghiordes knots are used to make pile, which you can imagine as a fuzzy surface on a fabric. Think of rugs with a cut-yarn surface to get an idea of the traditional use for this technique. Because we're weaving scarves that need to remain pliable to be practical, we used Ghiordes knots for tuffs of texture on a balanced-weave fabric. You can execute these knots several ways; the instructions here are for making a basic knot with cut lengths of yarn.

Making Ghiordes Knots

To create a Ghiordes knot, you'll need to weave a background of plain weave to have a stable fabric, and you'll need to cut lengths of yarn for making the knots (use a template to make faster work of this task).

Step 1. On a closed shed, insert the cut lengths—two 6" (15 cm) lengths are shown here—under 2 warp ends.

Step 2. Bring the ends together to one side, then use your finger to open the space between the 2 warp ends.

Step 3. Bring the 2 ends up through the center and pull down on the knot to secure it.

Step 4. Weave at least 2 picks of plain-weave ground to secure the knots.

Repeat Steps 1–4 as desired.

Note: *You can knot every 2 warp ends across the width for a very dense pile or spread out the knots, as we did for our Shaggy Scarf (page 102). The more knots, the denser the pile.*

Picked-Up Loops

Probably one of the fastest ways to make pile is with picked-up loops. You'll need two shuttles if you use different yarns for the background and for the pile.

Weaving Picked-Up Loops

You'll begin with a plain-weave background.

Step 1. Beginning from your dominant side (right to left shown here), open the shed and insert the looping weft all the way across the warp (we used a doubled weft here).

Step 2. Leaving the shed open, pick up loops by drawing them out of the shed between warp threads, placing them on a dowel or knitting needle (the bigger the knitting needle, the bigger the loop). Here, we picked up every other space on a U.S. size 10 (6 mm) knitting needle.

Step 3. Press down with the heddle.

Step 4. Carefully remove the knitting needle, beat again until firmly in place, then weave background for at least 2 picks.

Repeat Steps 1–4 as desired.

Helpful Hints

- ▶ It's easiest to work from your dominant side.
- ▶ You can pick up loops wherever you want; the more loops picked up, the denser the texture.
- ▶ The loops are not secure—they rely on the background weft for stability.
- ▶ Because the looping weft is woven from selvedge to selvedge, it will appear in the shed even in areas where no loops have been lifted.
- ▶ Cut the loops if desired.

The techniques presented in this chapter provide just a taste of the kinds of textures and patterns you can use to create unusual, surprising, and delightful results. We encourage you to explore on your own. Feel free to combine techniques, try others, or even make up your own.

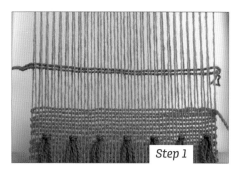

◀ Insert looping weft across the warp.

Step 1

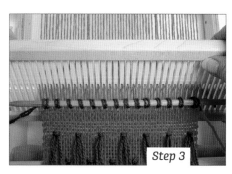

◀ Pick up the loops and place on a knitting needle.

Step 2

◀ Press down with the heddle.

Step 3

◀ Remove the knitting needle to leave loops on the surface.

Step 4

Warp floats are woven to create an open structure for a scarf that's both light and warm. Even though the structure looks delicate, the heavy finishing process fulls the yarns and prevents them from moving around afterwards. Note that the warp floats appear as weft floats on the reverse side.

SUN SHOWER

Combining fine novelty yarns and lace weave creates an open fabric that's both chic and light as a feather. In this design, warp floats help create a weightless, airy scarf. During the weaving, it will be hard to see the pattern. It only emerges after the fabric has been washed and the yarns pack together in some areas and leave other areas open. If you've never wielded a pick-up stick before, this is a perfect first project because it uses only one pick-up stick in the same pattern throughout the length of the scarf. We love the bits of sparkle and color that peek in and out of the fabric.

Designed by Jane Patrick | **Woven by** Betty Paepke

Finished size: 8" (20.5 cm) wide and 76" (193 cm) long, plus 4" (10 cm) fringe at each end.

Structure: Plain weave with warp floats.

Equipment: 10" (25.5 cm) wide, 8-dent rigid heddle reed; one stick shuttle; one pick-up stick.

Yarn: *Filatura di Crosa Superior* (70% cashmere, 25%/silk, 5% merino wool at 5,963 yd/lb [5,452 m/453 g]) in #73 Charcoal and #74 Grey Heather (both in warp only): 60 yd Charcoal and 36 yd Grey Heather (1 ball each at 328 yd [299 m]/25 g).

Filatura di Crosa Gioiello (30% kid mohair, 30% wool, 20% polyamide, 10% cotton, 10% polyester at 2,011 yd/lb [1,838 m/453 g] in #69 Tiger Eye (warp only): 72 yd (1 ball at 220 yd [201 m]/50 g).

Filatura di Crosa Nirvana (100% merino wool at 6,763 yd/lb [6,184 m/453 g]) in #35 Charcoal (warp and weft): 244 yd for weft and 42 yd for warp (1 ball at 372 yd [340 m]/25 g).

Warp length: 108" (274 cm), which allows 20" (51 cm) for loom waste and includes 8" (20 cm) for fringe—4" (10 cm) at each end.

Total warp ends: 70. *See note with draft if weaving this pattern on a shaft loom.*

Width in reed: Almost 9" (23 cm).

Ends per inch: 8.

Picks per inch: 10.

Yarn Wrapping

This yarn wrapping is shown actual size to assist you in making substitutions. Just place the yarn you want to use on top of the yarn chart to see if the yarn is the same size. Substituting a yarn with similar fiber content will be most successful.

Top to bottom:

➤ Filatura di Crosa Superior in #74 Grey Heather.

➤ Filatura di Crosa Superior #73 Charcoal.

➤ Filatura di Crosa Gioiello in #69 Tiger Eye.

➤ Firatura di Crosa Nirvana in #35 Charcoal.

Warping

Use the indirect method to measure the yarns on a warping board (see page 151). Before beginning to measure, we decided about what percentage of each yarn we wanted, then we measured them accordingly. We left each yarn on the warping board, then removed them all at once.

Wind 12 ends of Superior in Grey Heather, 20 ends of Superior in Charcoal, 14 ends of Nirvana, then 24 ends of Gioiello.

Thread the reed from the top of the stack of warp ends, placing them randomly across the weaving width. We threaded most of the Nirvana and all of the Superior Grey Heather in holes as shown at right.

Because we knew we'd want to pick-up the Superior Charcoal and Gioiello yarns, we threaded them in the slots, as well as in the remaining holes.

Threading a Mixed warp

Step 1

▲ Wind the yarns on top of one another, then remove them all at once.

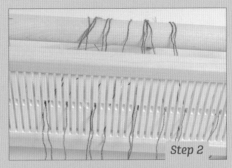
Step 2

▲ Working from the top of the stack, space the yarns randomly in the reed so that some are close together and others farther apart.

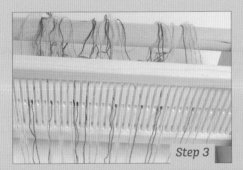
Step 3

▲ Thread most of the Nirvana and all of the Superior Grey Heather in the holes.

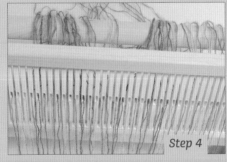
Step 4

▲ Thread the Superior Charcoal mostly in slots.

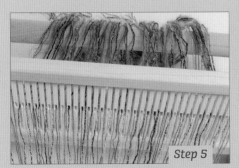
Step 5

◄ Thread the Gioiello mostly in slots.

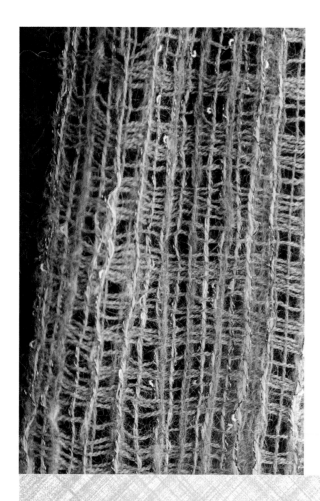

Weaving

Wind Nirvana on the stick shuttle.

Allow sufficient length in your front tie-on for a 4" (10 cm) fringe.

Leaving a tail four times the weaving width for hemstitching, weave 8 picks of plain weave.

Use the tail to hemstitch (see page 153) over 3 warp ends and 3 weft picks.

Follow the pick-up and weaving patterns as follows:

Pick-up pattern: 1 up, 1 down (see page 74).

Step 1. Down (place heddle in down position). Weave across.

Step 2. Up and pick-up stick (place heddle in up position and slide pick-up stick flat up to behind the heddle). Weave across.

Step 3. Down (place heddle in down position). Weave across.

Step 4. Up and pick-up stick (place heddle in up position and slide pick-up stick flat up to behind the heddle). Weave across.

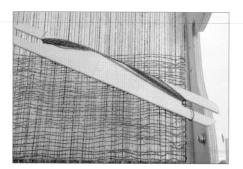

▲ *The fabric on the loom.*

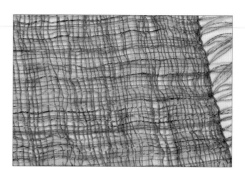

▲ *The pattern has not yet emerged, but there is a hint of it in this unwashed fabric.*

Step 5. Down (place heddle in down position). Weave across.

Step 6. Up (place heddle in up position). Weave across.

Repeat these 6 steps until the piece measures 85" (216 cm), being sure to leave sufficient length at the end for a 4" (10 cm) fringe.

Weave 8 picks plain weave.

Hemstitch over 3 warps and 3 wefts.

Note: *Because the weave is very loose, it will be difficult to see the pick-up pattern until the scarf is washed.*

Draft for Shaft Looms:

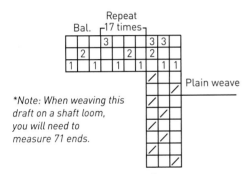

Note: When weaving this draft on a shaft loom, you will need to measure 71 ends.

Finishing

Remove the fabric from the loom, untying the knots in the front to allow for the fringe.

Handwash in very hot soapy water. Squeeze out excess water.

Place the scarf and a towel in the dryer on medium, checking often to monitor the amount of fulling (this is when the weave pattern will appear), keeping in mind that the fabric will be quite open.

Lightly steam-press the scarf and fringe using a pressing cloth.

Trim fringe to 4" (10 cm).

Variations

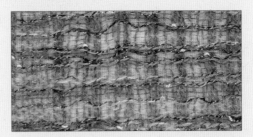

➤ Variation 1: This fabric is similar to our project except that we threaded it at 10 epi and wove shorter warp floats to create a lacy, but less open, fabric.

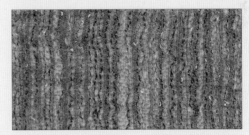

➤ Variation 2: Again, we used the same yarns for this swatch, except that it's sett at 12 epi and woven in plain weave with Superior in Charcoal.

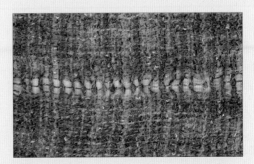

➤ Variation 3: Here, we used the same warp as the other two variations, but used Gioiello for the weft. A line of leno (see page 76) accents the otherwise plain fabric. The sett is 10 epi.

Designed by Cei Lambert

This lavender-colored scarf is bouncy with thermal properties because of its thickness. A mock waffle weave structure created by single warp and weft floats gives the fabric a lot of depth and a thick hand that makes this scarf very cozy.

LAVENDER LACE

Pick-up patterns create longer floats than in plain-weave fabrics. These longer floats result in thicker fabrics that generally have more drape. Weaving a pattern with both warp and weft floats, as we've done for this scarf, creates a fabric that looks pretty much the same on both sides. Be sure to use a light hand when beating the weft so it doesn't pack in too tightly and create a dense fabric.

Designed by Jane Patrick | **Woven by** Cei Lambert

Finished size: 6" (15 cm) wide and 70" (178 cm) long, plus 1" (2.5 cm) fringe at each end.

Structure: Mock waffle weave with plain-weave borders.

Equipment: 10" (25.5 cm) wide, 10-dent rigid heddle reed; one pick-up stick; one stick shuttle or slim boat shuttle with bobbin; tapestry needle.

Yarn: *Koigu Premium Merino* (100% merino wool at 1,554 yd/lb [1,420 m/453 g]) in #2501 Purple (warp and weft): 450 yd (3 skeins at 170 yd [155 m]/50 g).

Warp length: 104" (264 cm), which allows 24" (61 cm) for loom waste and includes 2" (5 cm) of fringe—1" (2.5 cm) at each end.

Total warp ends: 80.
Note: If weaving this pattern on a shaft loom, there will be 79 ends.

Width in reed: 8" (20.5 cm).

Ends per inch: 10.

Picks per inch: 10.

Yarn Wrapping

This yarn wrapping is shown actual size to assist you in making substitutions. Just place the yarn you want to use on top of the yarn chart to see if the yarn is the same size. Substituting a yarn with similar fiber content will be most successful.

➤ Koigu Premium Merino in #2501 Purple

Warping

Use the direct peg method (page 146).

Weaving

Wind Premium Merino on the stick shuttle or on a bobbin to use with a slim boat shuttle.

Leave 1" (2.5 cm) space from the apron rod for fringe.

Leaving a tail four times the weaving width for hemstitching, weave plain weave for 1" (2.5 cm).

Use the tail to hemstitch (see page 153) over 3 warp ends and 3 weft picks.

Place the heddle in the down position and use the pick-up stick to pick up: 1 up, 1 down, 1 up, 1 down, and so on across the width of the warp; being careful to pick up the warp ends behind the heddle.

Weave the length of the scarf as follows:

Pick-up pattern: 1 up, 1 down (see page 74).

Step 1. Up (place heddle in the up position). Weave across.

Step 2. Pick-up stick (place heddle in the neutral position, slide the pick-up stick close behind the heddle, and turn it on its side to create weft floats). Weave across.

Step 3. Up (place heddle in the up position). Weave across.

Step 4. Down (place heddle in the down position). Weave across.

Step 5. Up and pick-up stick (place the heddle in the up position and slide the pick-up stick flat— don't turn it on its edge—close behind the heddle to create warp floats). Weave across.

Step 6. Down (place heddle in the down position). Weave across.

Repeat these 6 steps until the piece measures about 79" (200.5 cm) or to the end of the warp.

Weave plain weave for 1" (2.5 cm).

Hemstitch over 3 warps and 3 wefts.

Note: *This pattern will be most successful if you aim for a balanced weave. You can achieve balance by bringing the heddle forward and gently pressing the pick into place. Do not "beat" the weft—doing so will result in a too-dense fabric.*

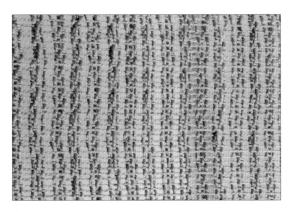

▲ *The weave will look very open on the loom but will full during the finishing process.*

Draft for shaft looms:

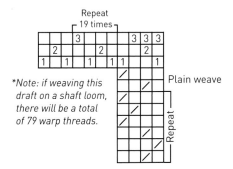

Note: if weaving this draft on a shaft loom, there will be a total of 79 warp threads.

Finishing

Remove the fabric from the loom, cutting close to the apron rod to allow for fringe.

Handwash in very hot water with a mild detergent or dish soap such as Dawn.

Rinse thoroughly and lay flat to dry.

If desired, steam-press on medium-high heat.

Trim fringe to 1" (2.5 cm).

Variations

➤ Variation 1: A red weft shows off the weave structure in a pronounced way. The warp and pick-up pattern are the same.

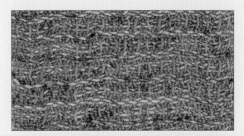

➤ Variation 2: The same warp and pick-up patterns are used here, but a heavily spaced-dyed yarn gives a mottled effect that obscures the weave structure.

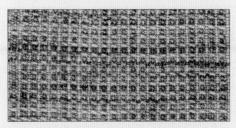

➤ Variation 3: The same yarns but in a different colorway are used for both the warp and weft in this sample. The weft was beaten tighter to produce a thicker fabric with less drape.

Designed by Jane Patrick

lavender lace

Spanish lace, a finger-controlled weave, is the basis for this scarf design. By pulling the wefts in each section to open up holes in the cloth, a dramatic lace pattern is created.

EYELET SCARF

Essentially, woven fabric is a grid of crossing verticals and horizontals. There's something comforting in this rigidity, and as weavers we love the process of laying in the horizontal wefts between the vertical warps. Sometimes, though, it's nice to bend the yarns, so to speak. Believe it or not, you can create cloth with curves. Woven in fine soft yarns, this scarf is heavily fulled after weaving to create a soft hand. Vintage beads and pearls in the fringe give this delicate scarf a little weight.

Designed and woven by Stephanie Flynn Sokolov

Finished size: 6" (15 cm) wide and 67" (170 cm) long, plus 10" (25.5 cm) of fringe at each end.

Structure: Spanish lace.

Equipment: 10" (25.5 cm) wide, 12-dent rigid heddle reed; one stick shuttle; tapestry needle; tapestry beater; needle threader; six dozen pearl and crystal beads in sizes ranging from 3, 5, 6, and 8mm. You can substitute clear and cream seed beads in a variety of sizes. We like the effect of the sparkle of glass beads; faceted beads would be ideal.

Yarn: *Classic Elite Silky Alpaca Lace* (70% alpaca, 30% silk at 4,000 yd/ lb [3,657 m/453 g]) in #2460 Wheatfield (warp only): 275 yd (1 ball at 440 yd [402 m]/50 g] ball).

Classic Elite Pirouette (67% kid mohair, 25% bamboo, 8% nylon at 4,475 yd/ lb [3,092 m/453 g] in #4050 Straw (weft only): 180 yd (1 ball at 246 yd [224 m]/50 g).

Warp length: 100" (254 cm), which allows 24" (61 cm) for loom waste and includes 20" (51 cm) for fringe—10" (25.5 cm) at each end.

Total warp ends: 109.

Width in reed: 9" (23 cm).

Ends per inch: 12.

Picks per inch: 9.

Yarn Wrapping

This yarn wrapping is shown actual size to assist you in making substitutions. Just place the yarn you want to use on top of the yarn chart to see if the yarn is the same size. Substituting a yarn with similar fiber content will be most successful.

Top to bottom:

➤ Classic Elite Silky Alpaca Lace in #2460 Wheatfield.

➤ Classic Elite Pirouette in #4050 Straw.

Warping

With Silky Alpaca and starting at the apron bar in the back, use the direct peg method (page 146) to thread the reed, ending the last warp end at the peg. This allows for an uneven number of warp ends with both selvedge ends threaded in holes.

Weaving

Wind Pirouette on the stick shuttle.

Allow sufficient length in your front tie-on for a 10" (25.5 cm) fringe.

Leaving a tail four times the weaving width for hemstitching and beginning with the heddle in the up position and the shuttle traveling from the right to the left, weave 3 picks and beat firmly to compact them together.

Use the tail to hemstitch (see page 153) over 3 warp ends and 3 weft picks.

Weave 9 picks of plain weave, then weave Spanish lace as follows:

Step 1. On the next up shed, put the shuttle through the first 7 up threads, pull the shuttle out of the shed, close the shed and beat back gently—this forms the first pick of the Spanish lace pattern.

Step 2. Change the shed and weave back under 7 up threads to the selvedge—this forms the second pick of the pattern and should be pulled slightly to create a gap in the warp ends.

Step 3. Continue building up the first section of the Spanish lace pattern in the same way for a total of 6 picks.

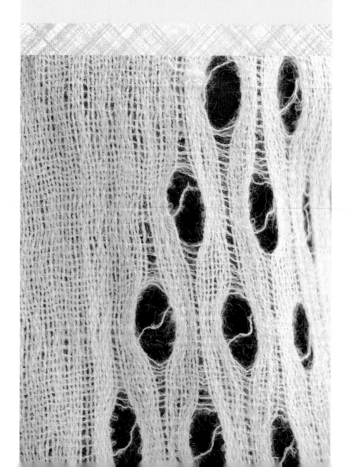

Step 4. On the next (7th) pick, bring the shuttle under the next 10 up warp threads that have not been worked (a total of 17 raised threads from the selvedge).

Step 5. Close the shed and beat with a tapestry beater.

This traveling thread will be your first pick on the new section.

► Put the shuttle under the first 7 up threads.

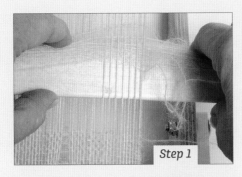

Step 1

◄ Weave back under 7 up threads of the next shed.

Step 2a

► Pull on the weft to create a gap in the warp ends.

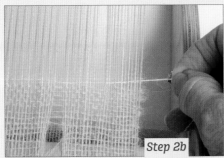

Step 2b

◄ Weave this section for a total of 6 picks.

Step 3

► For the 7th pick, bring the shuttle under 17 up threads (7 from the first group plus the next 10).

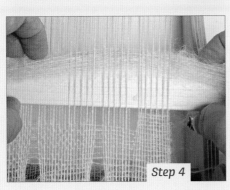

Step 4

◄ Close the shed and beat with a tapestry beater.

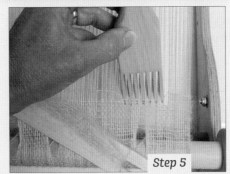

Step 5

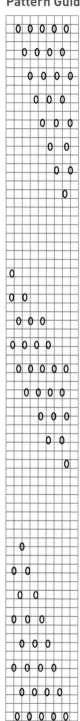

1 square = 1 inch

Now build up the weaving in this second section, working only these 10 up threads.

Follow the pattern guide at left, working the required number of holes across the warp and weaving 9 picks from selvedge to selvedge between pattern rows.

End with 9 picks to balance the first end of the scarf.

Hemstitch over 3 warps and 3 wefts.

Note: *Weaving this pattern requires duplicity in tension. When you weave a row of the Spanish lace pattern, you'll want to pull the weft tightly to create the holes. For the plain-weave sections, on the other hand, you must use very little tension on the weft to maintain consistent draw-in and even selvedges.*

Finishing

Remove the fabric from the loom, untying the knots in the front to allow for the fringe.

Handwash in very warm water, gently agitating the fabric. Then rub vigorously in both directions around the holes. Gently wring out.

Place the scarf and a towel in the dryer on the low setting for 15 minutes or until dry, checking the progress every 5 minutes to prevent over-fulling.

Steam-press using a pressing cloth.

Trim the fringe to 10" (25.5 cm), using a ruler, rotary cutter, and healing mat.

Thread beads and pearls on the warp ends as desired, using a needle threader to help bring the warp threads through the beads and securing them in place with overhand knots. Tie bundles of 5 warp ends each in overhand knots about 5" (12.5 cm) from the hemstitching.

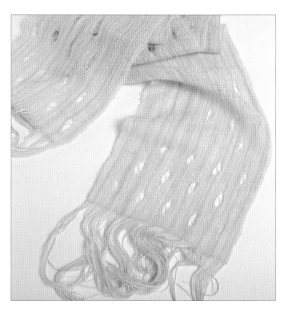

▲ *Scarf prior to washing.*

Variation

➤ A simplified version of Spanish lace is used as an accent along the length of this otherwise plain scarf. Yarns are Classic Elite Silky Alpaca in #2432 Garnet and Classic Elite Pirouette in #4023 Red Coral sett at 12 epi.

Designed by Sara Goldenberg White

When you first look at this scarf it's hard to know what's going on, except that it looks intriguing. This leno variation, while simple to weave, looks complicated. Even though this finger-controlled weave takes time, the wide sett of 5 epi makes the weaving relatively fast.

LATTICE SCARF

This scarf is an example of how you can take a basic technique and combine it with an interesting yarn for fantastic results. Leno is perfect for this lattice scarf because it literally twists warp yarns that "lock" the weft yarn into place, creating a stable, yet open fabric. This variation on traditional leno creates a crisscross look. The yarn choice "makes" the scarf, both for its long space-dyed coloration and its structure—a lightweight, slightly felted singles yarn. You'll look like an expert when you wear this scarf (and you don't have to reveal the secret of how it's made)!

Designed and woven by Stephanie Flynn Sokolov

Finished size: 5½" (14 cm) wide and 70" (178 cm) long, plus 4" (10 cm) fringe at each end.

Structure: Leno variation.

Equipment: 10" (25.5 cm) wide, 5-dent rigid heddle reed; one stick shuttle; one pick-up stick; tapestry beater; tapestry needle.

Yarn: *Skacel Schoppel Pur* (hand-dyed, slightly felted merino wool singles at 745 yd/ lb [681 m/453 g]) in #1507 red/brown/blue mix (warp and weft): 145 yd (1 skein at 164 yd [149 m]/100 g).

Warp length: 92" (233.5 cm), which allows for 18" (45.5 cm) of loom waste and includes 8" (20 cm) for fringe—4" (10 cm) at each end.

Total warp ends: 44.

Width in reed: 9" (23 cm).

Ends per inch: 5.

Picks per inch: 2 per 1.5" (3.8 cm), or ¾" (2 cm) apart.

Yarn Wrapping

This yarn wrapping is shown actual size to assist you in making substitutions. Just place the yarn you want to use on top of the yarn chart to see if the yarn is the same size. Substituting a yarn with similar fiber content will be most successful.

➤ Skacel Schoppel Pur in #1507 red/brown/blue mix.

Variations

➤ Variation 1: This variation, woven by Stephanie Flynn Sokolov, is from the same skein as the one used for the project. Very long color sections in the yarn cause this swatch to look quite different.

➤ Variation 2: Pur in #1993 purple/pink/brown mix is used for the warp, but it's crossed instead with a worsted-weight wool, which further enhances the helix effect of the twisted warps.

Woven by Stephanie Flynn Sokolov

Warping

Using the direct peg method (page 146), start winding at the boundary between two colors. For the yarn to move through the length of the warp much like a double helix pattern, keep the warp length to 92" (234 cm).

Weaving

Wind Schoppel Pur on the stick shuttle.

Allow sufficient length in your front tie-on for a 4" (10 cm) fringe. Leaving a tail four times the width in the reed for hemstitching, weave 3 picks, then beat firmly to compact them together.

Use the tail to hemstitch (see page 153) over 3 warp ends and 3 weft picks.

Use the Jane Variation of 2/2 leno on a closed shed (see page 101) in which 6 warp ends are included in the twists as follows:

Working right to left will be most natural if you're right-handed (you can work this technique left to right if that is more comfortable for you).

Step 1. With the shuttle on the right side and with the shed closed, use your right hand to pick up warp ends 1 and 2, then lift them over ends 5 and 6, skipping ends 3 and 4.

Step 2. Place the pick-up stick under ends 5 and 6 and over 1 and 2.

Pick up warp ends 3 and 4 and lift them over threads 9 and 10, skipping threads 7 and 8. Then insert the pick-up stick under threads 9 and 10 and over 3 and 4.

Continue in this pattern across the entire warp.

Step 3. Turn the pick-up stick on edge and insert the shuttle from right to left. Adjust the warp threads to even them out if they bunch up.

Step 4. Place the heddle in the up position and weave across from left to the right.

Repeat these 4 steps until 70" (178 cm) have been woven.

Weave 3 picks and beat firmly to compact them together.

Hemstitch over 3 warps and 3 wefts.

Note: *Because the twists in the warp make it difficult to use the heddle to beat the weft, you may find a tapestry beater helpful to press the weft to within ¾" (2 cm) of the last pick.*

Finishing

Remove the scarf from the loom, untying the knots in front to allow for fringe.

Steam-press using a press cloth.

Trim the fringe to 4" (10 cm), using a ruler, rotary cutter, and healing mat.

For future cleaning, soak the scarf in soapy water, rinse, then lay flat to dry, shaping the scarf as you might a sweater.

THe Jane variation

◄ *Pick up warp ends 1 and 2 and lift them over ends 5 and 6, skipping ends 3 and 4.*

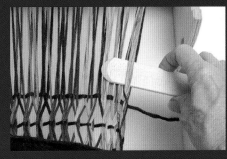

◄ *Place the pick-up stick under ends 5 and 6 and over ends 1 and 2.*

◄ *Turn the pick-up stitch on edge and insert the shuttle from right to left.*

◄ *Place the heddle in the up position and insert the shuttle from left to right.*

A springy wool is sett at
10 epi and accented with
single ends of mohair
for vertical stripes along
the length of this scarf.
Ghiordes knots in three
bright hues punctuate
the ends.

SHAGGY SCARF

Adding texture to a scarf is such a weaverly thing to do. For this scarf, we used a traditional rug-pile technique for tufted accoutrements at the ends. Ghiordes knots have been used for centuries for Middle Eastern and Swedish rya rugs. Here, knots are tied on a balanced plain-weave ground at both ends of the scarf. Knots are tied on both the front and back for a totally reversible piece.

Designed and woven by Jane Patrick

Finished size: 7¾" (19.5 cm) wide and 70" (178 cm) long, plus 1" (2.5 cm) fringe at each end.

Structure: Plain weave with Ghiordes knots tied on the front and back.

Equipment: 10" (25.5 cm) wide, 10-dent rigid heddle reed; one stick shuttle; 6" (15 cm) strip of file folder folded in half to yield a 3" (7.5 cm) wide strip to use as template for cutting yarn for Ghiordes knots; scissors.

Yarn: *Louet Gems Fingering Weight* (100% worsted wool at 1,750 yd/lb [1,600 m/453 g]) in Goldilocks (warp and weft): 466 yd (3 skeins at 185 yd [169 m]/50 g).

Louet Worsted Weight Mohair (78% mohair, 13% wool, 9% nylon at 946 yd/lb [865 m/453 g]) in:

◆ Sunflower (warp and weft): 65 yd (1 skein at 105 yd [96 m]/50 g).

◆ Lichen (weft only): 30 yd (1 skein).

◆ Aqua Marine (weft only): 21 yd (1 skein).

Warp length: 96" (244 cm), which includes 18" (45.5 cm) for loom waste and allows 2" (5 cm) of fringe—1" (2.5 cm) at each end.

Total warp ends: 99.

Width in reed: 10" (25.5 cm).

Ends per inch: 10.

Picks per inch: 10.

Yarn Wrapping

This yarn wrapping is shown actual size to assist you in making substitutions. Just place the yarn you want to use on top of the yarn chart to see if the yarn is the same size. Substituting a yarn with similar fiber content will be most successful.

Top to bottom:

➤ Louet Gems Fingering Weight in Goldilocks.

➤ Louet Worsted Weight Mohair in Sunflower.

➤ Louet Worsted Weight Mohair in Lichen.

➤ Louet Worsted Weight Mohair in Aqua Marine.

▼ *Wrap the mohair around a 6" (15 cm) strip of file folder that's been folded to yield a 3" (7.5 cm) width. Use sharp scissors to cut between the two pieces of folder (along the nonfolded side) to make equal lengths for the Ghiordes knots.*

Warping

Using the indirect warping method (see page 151), follow the warping plan below.

Warping Plan

		Repeat 13 times			
Gems, Goldilocks	10*		5		10	85
Worsted Mohair, Sunflower		1		1		14
Total Ends						99

Begin in a slot, being careful to thread all mohair warp yarns in a slot.

Weaving

Wrap the mohair around the 3" (7.5 cm) file folder template as a guide for cutting 6" (15 cm) lengths. Slip scissors between the two pieces of file folder and cut one side of the wrapped yarns to make 6" (15 cm) lengths. You'll need 168 lengths of Sunflower, 128 lengths of Aqua Marine, and 184 lengths of Lichen.

Wind Gems Fingering on the stick shuttle.

Allow sufficient length in your front tie-on for a 1" (2.5 cm) fringe.

Leaving a tail four times the width in the reed for hemstitching, weave 12 picks.

Use the tail to hemstitch (see page 153) over 4 warp ends and 2 weft picks.

First Border

Step 1. Beginning with the 2 warps to the *right* of the first mohair warp end, tie 2 strands of green mohair into a Ghiordes knot (see page 107). Continue across the piece, tying a knot on the 2 warp ends to the right of all the remaining mohair warp ends, following the color order at right. Reversing the colors, tie another set of knots at the same place as the previous knots, but bring the yarn ends to the back of the fabric (alternatively, you can turn the loom over to work the knots on the reverse side)—there are fourteen knots on each side in the first row.

Step 2. Weave 10 picks of plain weave with Gems Fingering.

Step 3. Make a second row of knots, this time working the knots over the 2 warp threads to the *left* of each mohair warp end.

Step 4. Weave 10 picks of plain weave with Gems Fingering.

Step 5. Make a third row of knots, starting to the *right* of the mohair warp ends.

Step 6. Weave 10 picks of plain weave with Gems Fingering.

Step 7: Make a fourth row of knots on the *left* side of the mohair warp ends, skipping every other mohair warp for a total of seven knots.

Step 8. Weave 10 picks of plain weave with Gems Fingering.

Step 9. Make a fifth row of knots, skipping the first mohair warp, make a knot on the *right* side of the second mohair warp end, then skip every other mohair warp to make a total of seven knots.

Step 10. Weave 10 picks of plain weave with Gems Fingering.

Step 11. Make a sixth row of knots, beginning on the *left* side of the first warp end, skipping 2 mohair warps, then tying a knot on the left side of the fourth mohair warp, and so on across the warp for a total of five knots.

Step 12. Weave 10 picks of plain weave with Gems Fingering.

Step 13. Make a seventh row of knots, beginning on the right side of the third mohair warp end, then skip 2 mohair warps, tying a knot, and so on for a total of four knots.

color order for ghiordes knots

First Knot Row
▶ **Front side:** *Green, blue; repeat from *.
▶ **Back side:** *Blue, green; repeat from * (in other words, wherever there's a green knot on the front, tie a blue knot on the back, and vice versa).

Second Knot Row
▶ **Front side:** *Yellow, blue, green; repeat from *.
▶ **Back side:** *Blue, green, yellow; repeat from *.

Third Knot Row
▶ **Front side:** *Green, yellow, green, blue, yellow, green*, yellow, blue; repeat from * to * once.
▶ **Back side:** *Yellow, green, yellow, blue, green, yellow*, green, blue; repeat from * to * once.

Fourth Knot Row
▶ **Front side:** Yellow, green, yellow, blue, green, yellow, green.
▶ **Back side:** Green, yellow, green, blue, yellow, green, yellow.

Fifth Knot Row
▶ **Front side:** Yellow, yellow, green, yellow, yellow, green, yellow.
▶ **Back side:** Green, green, yellow, green, green, yellow, green.

Sixth Knot Row
▶ **Front side:** Yellow.
▶ **Back side:** Green.

Seventh Knot Row
▶ **Front side:** Yellow.
▶ **Back side:** Green.

◄ Weaving in progress.

◄ You may find it helpful to use a tapestry beater to press the knots into place.

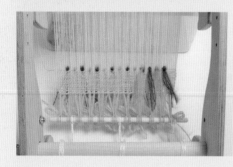

◄ The reverse side of the fabric on the loom.

Variation

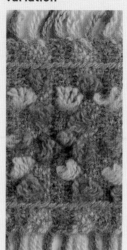

➤ Instead of leaving the fringe long, cut the knots short for a dotted look. For this sample, we used a striped warp for an interesting background for the rows of knots. These yarns are all alpaca-blend fingering yarn from North Light Fibers, in Bark Brown, Island Meadow Buttercup, Sky Blue Lace, and Salmon.

Designed by Jane Patrick

Center
Weave plain weave at 10 ppi for 62" (157.5 cm).

Second Border
Beginning with Step 13, repeat the steps for the previous border in reverse order, ending with Step 1. After the last row of knots, weave 12 picks and hemstitch over 4 warp ends and 2 weft picks.

Finishing
Remove the fabric from the loom, untying the knots in the front to allow for the fringe.

Handwash in very hot water with mild detergent. Rinse in warm water.

Place the scarf and a bath towel in a dryer on the medium-hot setting until dry, checking every 5 minutes to monitor progress.

Steam-press with a medium-hot iron.

Use your fingers to smooth the fringe and the Ghiordes knots.

Trim the fringe to 1" (2.5 cm).

How to make a Ghiordes knot with cut ends

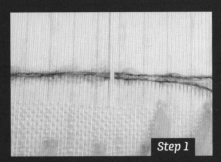

Step 1

Step 2

Step 3

▲ Place a length of yarn under 2 warp ends. Bring the 2 ends together and pull to the side.

▲ Separate the 2 warp ends with your finger, then bring the loose yarn ends up through the center space between the separated warp ends.

▲ Pull down on the ends to tighten the knot.

How to make a "Reverse" Ghiordes knot with cut ends

This process is worked much the same as for making regular Ghiordes knots, but the ends are pulled to the back of the fabric.

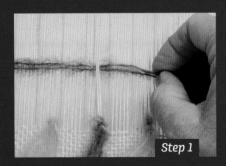

Step 1

Step 2

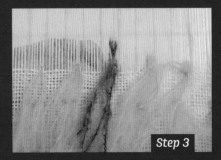

Step 3

▲ Place a length of yarn under 2 warp ends. Bring the 2 ends together.

▲ Separate the 2 warp ends, then bring the loose yarn ends down through the center space between the separated warp ends and to the back side of the fabric.

▲ Pull down on the ends to tighten the knot.

shaggy scarf

4 Altered surfaces

In this chapter, we explore how far you can take the weaving experience to create truly stunning, inventive, and original scarves. Except for the Fringy Collar (page 132), which has a pile surface created with Ghiordes knots and laid-in fabric strips, and the Peter Pan Collar (page 120), which features hemstitching, all of the projects in this chapter were woven in plain weave. It's the yarns and their spacing in the warp and weft, combined with various finishing techniques, that turn a plain-weave fabric into gorgeous cloth.

Fulling

For many of our scarves, we used heavy fulling, which is a process for finishing wool fibers. Fulling causes the fibers to bloom and fill the spaces between adjacent warp ends and weft picks. Taken to an extreme (and called felting), the fibers actually glom onto each other to thicken and shrink the fabric, which takes the process to the point at which the woven structure is completely obscured. If you've ever accidentally felted a sweater in the washing machine, you get the idea. Needless to say, once felted, there's no going back.

If you want your scarf to felt, choose nonsuperwash wool, wool blend, alpaca, and mohair yarns. Read the yarn labels carefully when you choose wool yarns—those that are labeled as "superwash" or "washable" have been treated to prevent fulling. No matter how hard you try, these yarns will not felt.

Wool felts readily. If you looked at a length of wool fiber under a microscope, you'd see little barbs along the length of each fiber. When subjected to heat, moisture, agitation, and detergent, these barbs grab onto each other (and once they grab on, they don't let go) to make the fabric denser, thicker, and warmer.

If you plan to heavily full a woven scarf, keep in mind that the farther apart the warp and weft yarns are (i.e., the more "open" the weave), the more the fabric will shrink. This shrinkage occurs because the yarns have to move farther before they can grab onto each other, closing up larger spaces to tighten the fabric.

By using fulling as a means to create stable and lightweight fabrics, you can expand the range of rigid heddle looms. Unless you add a second heddle (which is beyond the scope of this book), the sett in a rigid heddle loom is limited by the 12-dent (i.e., 12 ends per inch, abbreviated epi) reed, which is typically considered too "open" for fine yarns. If you heavily full the fabric after weaving, you can use finer yarns without sacrificing fabric stability. However, when you design a scarf, remember that heavy fulling may cause the fabric to shrink 30% or more! You'll need to adjust the weaving length and width accordingly.

In the case of our Spaced and Felted Scarf (page 110), we used a fine wool-silk yarn and left spaces in the reed and in the weaving to create holes. The fabric looked open and "thready" when it came off the loom. During the finishing process, the woven areas "knitted" together and the nonwoven areas opened up even more. As you can see, the result is that even though the fabric has a lot of open spaces, it's quite stable and beautifully wearable because the yarns felted together.

For our Felt Resist Bananagram Scarf (page 124), we used a different felting technique. We wove with very fine yarn, then used rubber bands to secure small plastic tiles along the fabric. After fulling the scarf heavily, we removed the tiles to reveal unfulled mounds that stand in relief against the rest of the fabric, which shrank considerably. The tile shapes are permanent in the finished fabric.

Another intriguing technique is differential shrinkage, in which yarns that felt are purposefully combined with yarns that don't felt, as you can see in our Gypsy Dancer Scarf (page 116). Even a hint of felting can provide shaping, as it does along the edges of our Peter Pan Collar (page 120).

Although not for visual drama, we also used heavy fulling for our Recycled Sweater Scarf (page 128), which combines a nonfelting superwash wool in the warp and fine cashmere (raveled from an old sweater) in the weft. Without fulling, the weaving would have been too open to be stable.

Energized Yarns

Although our Metamorphosis Scarf (page 136) may look like it's been felted, its texture is the result of a fine, over-twisted wool yarn (treated with a sizing agent to make it manageable) in the weft combined with a fine silk in the warp. On the loom, the surface is smooth, but once the sizing is washed out, the over-twist is activated and the fabric "collapses." It does so much the way a spring that's stretched straight springs back when the tension is released. If you happen to be a handspinner, you can create your own over-twisted yarns or add additional twist to a commercial yarn to produce similar results.

Dye and Discharge

Another way to achieve unique results is to treat the fabric or the yarns before weaving by painting, dip dyeing, or tie-dyeing the yarns or fabric to create pattern and surface interest. You can also remove color, as we did with our Steampunk Scarf (page 140). After weaving and finishing the fabric for this scarf, we used a bleach pen with stencil patterns to remove the color. You could create layer-on-layer color patterning by dyeing the yarns before weaving, then removing some of the color afterward.

We encourage you to explore these ideas further through your own experimentation. Our mantra of "sample, sample, sample" applies to testing various setts, yarn combinations, and finishing techniques. You'll only know if you're on track to create a scarf with the right drape, look, and finish if you test your ideas in a sample. Although we wove all of these scarves on a 10" or 15" (25.5 or 38 cm) Cricket loom, you can increase your possibilities by adding a second heddle (see Jane's *A Weaver's Idea Book* or her video Rigid Heddle Weaving for more on using two heddles) or by using a shaft loom.

We hope, in the end, that our "inspired scarves" truly move you to try the techniques in these pages, as well as to pursue your own ideas and designs.

A fine spaced-dyed silk-wool blend yarn is the star of our Spaced and Felted Scarf. Impress your friends with this piece that looks tricky but is so simple to weave.

SPACED AND FELTED SCARF

When you look at this scarf on the loom, you'll find it hard to believe that it's the same fabric as the finished piece shown here. The final scarf is impressive, but it's really (really!) quite easy to achieve these results. A fine wool-silk blend space-dyed yarn is used for warp and weft. The sett is 12 epi with spaces left unthreaded in the heddle as well as spacers inserted during the weaving. The beautiful pattern is achieved in part by the spaces in the warp. The fabric is felted by hand, transforming a loose, open weave to a woven grid that holds its shape and remains soft and flexible.

Designed and woven by Stephanie Flynn Sokolov

Finished size: 8" (20.5 cm) wide and 80" (203 cm) long.

Structure: Plain weave.

Equipment: 15" (38 cm) wide, 12-dent rigid heddle reed; one stick shuttle; spacers of varying widths (see page 112).

Yarn: *Lorna's Laces Helen's Lace* (50% tussah silk, 50% merino wool at 5,000 yd/lb [4,572 m/453 kg]) in #70 Vera (warp and weft): 550 yd (1 skein at 1,250 yd [1143 m]/4 oz.

Warp length: 120" (305 cm), which includes 24" (61 cm) for loom waste.

Total warp ends: 90.

Width in reed: 15" (38 cm).

Ends per inch: Spaced warp in a 12-dent reed.

Picks per inch: 8 in woven areas.

Yarn Wrapping

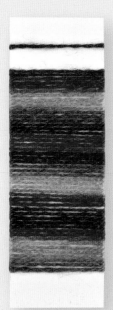

This yarn wrapping is shown actual size to assist you in making substitutions. Just place the yarn you want to use on top of the yarn chart to see if the yarn is the same size. Substituting a yarn with similar fiber content will be most successful.

➤ Lorna's Laces Helen's Lace in #70 Vera.

Warping

Using the direct peg method (page 146), follow the warping plan at right.

Note: *The direct warping technique will put 2 warp ends in each slot. After threading the slots and winding the warp onto the back beam, thread the holes; working from the right, thread one of the 2 threads in the first slot through the hole to the left. Finish threading this first group of eight threads (the first 4 slots) in the holes to the left. Thread the remainder of the scarf by taking 1 thread from each slot and threading into the hole to the right. This sequence begins and ends in a hole, which helps to keep the selvedges as even as possible while weaving with the spacers.*

We cut our spacers from poster board, cutting each 15¾" (40 cm) long (just a little longer than the weaving width). We cut the spacers to different widths to allow for variations in the size of the holes they produced.

Cut seven spacers, cutting some straight from edge to edge and tapering others between the two edges as described below. We numbered the spacers and used them in numerical order to ensure a variety of sizes of spaces between the groupings throughout the piece.

Spacer	Width at Left Side	Width at Right Side
1	1¼" (3.2 cm)	1¼" (3.2 cm)
2	¾" (2 cm)	¾" (2 cm)
3	½" (1.3 cm)	1½" (3.8 cm)
4	1" (2.5 cm)	1" (2.5 cm)
5	½" (1.3 cm)	1½" (3.8 cm)
6	1" (2.5 cm)	½" (1.3 cm)
7	¾" (2 cm)	¾" (2 cm)

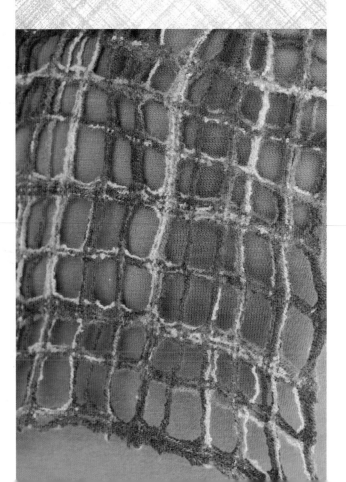

Warping Plan

Threaded slot	4		2		5		4		3		4		5		2		4		3		5		4	45
Empty slot		2		4		5		5		3		5		3		4		3		5		5		44
Total Slots																								**89**

Weaving

Wind Helen's Lace on the stick shuttle.

Because there is no fringe, start weaving as close to the apron rod as possible.

Leaving a tail four times the weaving width for hemstitching, weave 8 picks.

Use the tail to hemstitch (see page 153) over 3 warp ends and 3 weft picks.

Weave in a random pattern, varying the number of picks per section of weft between the spacers from 4 picks to 11 picks.

To hold the spaces during weaving, use the spacers in order from 1 to 7, inserting them into the last open shed of each woven section. Alternate the wide and narrow ends of the spacers as needed to keep the fell of the cloth straight. For example, if the wide end of the spacer is on the right, place the wide end of the next spacer on the left.

As you advance the warp, the spacers will start to roll over the breast beam. When this happens, release the tension slightly and remove the spacer closest to the cloth beam while holding onto the next spacer to minimize shifting of the warp threads.

Check to see that the warp threads have not escaped to a neighboring group when the spacers are removed. To help prevent escapees, squish the warp threads together with your fingers into their sections before winding on to the cloth beam. We found that if we squeezed the warp sections together on the fabric between the front beam

and the cloth beam, the fabric consistently kept its shape better.

Weave the piece as long as possible—you don't need to leave space for fringe.

End by weaving 8 picks.

Hemstitch over 3 warps and 3 wefts.

Finishing

Remove the fabric from the loom, cutting close to the apron rod and carefully unrolling the fabric from the cloth beam.

Take your time to finish this scarf and do not rush—the finishing process "makes" this piece. Plan 30 to 40 minutes for the felting process.

Roll the scarf around kraft paper or a paper towel tube to hold it.

Fill a sink half full of warm water and a splash of Dawn dish soap.

Starting at one end, roll out a length of the scarf and lay the width of the scarf across your arm between fingertip and elbow (this will help you see the definition of the holes you've woven and keep them in place while you gently rub back and forth between your fingertips, rubbing along the segment of the warp on your yarn, and then across the weft). Massage the junctions where the warp and weft cross with a circular motion to hold the yarns together. Add more soap if necessary to minimize the friction between your hands and the yarn. Too much friction will shift the yarn into the open spaces. Work your way up and down the length of the scarf several times.

When the yarn and the holes feel stable without shifting, rinse with warm water to remove some of the soap. This will increases the friction and the speed at which the scarf will felt. Rub the scarf back and forth on itself until the desired amount of felting is achieved (you can use a washboard to speed the process). Massage the scarf until the yarns felt together (we've found that different colors shrink at different rates).

Rinse and then wring out the excess water.

Lay flat to dry.

Steam-press.

Note: *We hemstitched the beginning and the end of the scarf. Because there are no warps in the exposed weft areas, we just looped over these areas with half hitches. This gives the ends a distinct line and holds the first and last ends from migrating during the finishing process.*

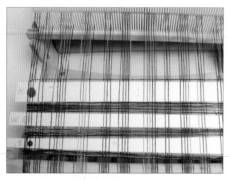

◄ *We used variably sized spacers between sections of weft to hold the spaces during weaving.*

◄ *The fabric off the loom but before felting.*

Variation

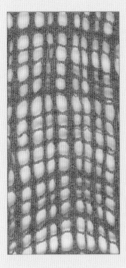

➤ We used Helen's Lace from Lorna's Laces in a solid color (Poppy) for this scarf and gave it a more vigorous felting treatment, creating a more industrial and modern—and less delicate—effect.

Designed by
Stephanie Flynn Sokolov

Fibers and yarns are blended to create the desired hand for this playful piece. The selvedges are accented with a shiny metallic and mohair yarn for a bit of sparkle and flair at the edges. Broad stripes of pink bamboo provide drape while the center stripe of alpaca felts to create surface interest. To give the desired hand and "tooth" to the fabric, we alternated one pick of bamboo with one pick of a laceweight wool/silk blend throughout the length.

GYPSY DANCER

Differential shrinkage means that some yarns will shrink more than others in the finishing process. When some yarns full more than others, the fabric will pucker to create a rippled effect. For this piece, we warped a broad stripe of alpaca along the center of the weaving, which we then heavily fulled to felt the yarns together. We used a washboard to agitate just the center stripe, leaving the mohair yarns at the selvedges to full, but not felt.

Designed and woven by Stephanie Flynn Sokolov

Finished size: 4¼" (11 cm) wide and 36" (91.5 cm) long, plus 6" (15 cm) of fringe at each end.

Note: This piece shrank 39% in length and 23% in width.

Structure: Plain weave with differential shrinkage.

Equipment: 10" (25.5 cm) wide, 12-dent rigid heddle reed; two stick shuttles; washboard (optional); 150 orange size 4mm beads (one for each warp end) for fringe accent (optional).

Yarn: *Plymouth Gold Rush* (80% rayon, 20% polyester at 2,000 yd/lb [1,828 m/453 g]) in #4 Bright Gold (warp only): 10 yd (1 tube at 110 yd [100 m]/259 g).

Louet North America Worsted Weight Mohair (78% mohair, 13% wool, 9% nylon at 946 yd/lb [865 m/453 g]) in #76 Sunflower (warp only): 10 yd (1 skein at 105 yd [96 m]/50 g).

Cotton Clouds Bambu 7 (100% bamboo at 2,100 yd/lb [1,920 m/453 g]) in #136 Magenta (warp and weft): 220 yd (1 cone at 525 yd [480 m]/4 oz).

Plymouth Baby Alpaca (100% baby alpaca at 3,995 yd/lb [3,653 m/453 g] in color #2055 rust (warp only): 38 yd (1 skein at 437 yd [359 m]/50 g).

Lorna's Laces Helen's Lace (50% tussah silk, 50% merino wool at 5,000 yd/lb [4,572 m/453 g]) in Courage (weft only): 70 yd (1 skein at 1,250 yd [1,143 m]/4 oz).

Warp length: 85" (216 cm), which includes 24" (61 cm) of loom waste and 6" (15 cm) of fringe at each end.

Total warp ends: 75.

Width in reed: 6¼" (16 cm).

Ends per inch: 12.

Picks per inch: 11 to 12.

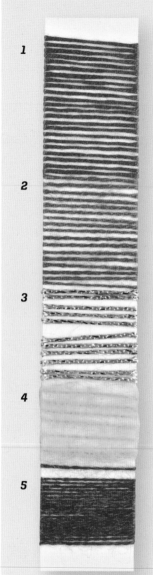

Yarn Wrapping

This yarn wrapping is shown actual size to assist you in making substitutions. Just place the yarn you want to use on top of the yarn chart to see if the yarn is the same size. Substituting a yarn with similar fiber content will be most successful.

Top to bottom:

➤ **1.** Cotton Clouds Bambu 7 in #136 Magenta.

➤ **2.** Lorna's Laces Helen's Lace in Courage.

➤ **3.** Plymouth Gold Rush in #4 Bright Gold.

➤ **4.** Louet North America Worsted Weight Mohair in #76 Sunflower.

➤ **5.** Plymouth Baby Alpaca in #2055 Rust.

Warping

Use the direct peg method (page 146) as follows:

1 slot with Worsted Weight Mohair.

1 slot with Gold Rush.

13 slots with Bambu 7.

8 slots with Baby Alpaca.

13 slots with Bambu 7, but end at the peg in the last slot for a total of 25 ends.

1 slot with Gold Rush.

1 slot with Worsted Weight Mohair.

To thread the reed, start with the mohair and sley it in the first 2 slots. Remove both gold threads from the slot and sley them in the holes. Beginning and ending in this way allows the mohair to be in the slots nearest the selvedges and gives it a little extra room to move around. The gold yarn threaded in between the strands of mohair yarn helps alleviate the fuzzy mohair tendrils from sticking to their neighbors (to make sure that the selvedges are threaded in this way, we measured an uneven number of warp ends).

Weaving

Wind Helen's Lace and Bambu 7 on separate stick shuttles. Allow sufficient length in your front tie-on for a 6" (15 cm) fringe.

Leaving a tail four times the weaving width for hemstitching, weave 3 picks of Helen's Lace.

Use the tail to hemstitch (see page 153) over 2 warp ends and 3 weft picks.

Alternate 1 pick of each yarn to the end of the warp, allowing for 6" (15 cm) of fringe at the end.

With Helen's Lace, weave 3 picks, then hemstitch over 2 warps and 3 wefts.

▲ *The weave is very open on the loom.*

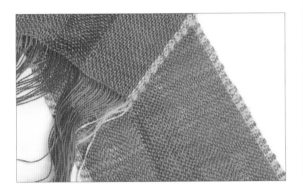

▲ *The fabric off the loom and before finishing.*

Felting woven Fabric

For a fabric to felt, you'll need warm water, soap, and agitation. All three ingredients are equally important. Initially, the soap helps to reduce the surface tension of the water to speed up the wetting. The first agitation of the fabric needs to be gentle to ensure that the felting happens evenly across the fabric without shifting the weave. A little extra soap helps to reduce the friction that keeps the fabric stable, but it also slows the felting process. When the fabric looks like the weave is moving closer together, splash some water on the fabric to remove a little soap and agitate some more. Add soap a little at a time and continue agitating. Once the fibers have moved close enough for the structure to look solid, continue rubbing hard, adding and removing soap until the fabric ceases to shrink any further. Rinse the remaining soap from the fabric and hang to dry.

Finishing

Remove the fabric from the loom, untying the knots in front to allow for fringe.

Submerge in very warm water with a dash of Dawn dish soap and let soak for 10 minutes.

When the water reaches a comfortable temperature, gently rub the alpaca stripe in the center of the warp.

Add a little dish soap directly to the alpaca stripe and continue to rub.

When this section begins to shrink and creates a ruffle, start adding some elbow grease—using a washboard if desired—to speed up the process, rubbing hard until the stripe no longer shrinks.

Rinse in warm water and squeeze out excess moisture.

Hang to dry.

Use an iron and pressing cloth to add softness and sheen to the ruffled edges.

Straighten the fringe and press flat under a pressing cloth.

If desired, add one bead to each strand of the fringe, placing the beads randomly by tying an overhand knot below the beads.

Brush the selvedges to lift the nap on the mohair.

Dress up a simple dress or finely knitted sweater with this little woven collar. Ladder hemstitching worked along the length of the scarf creates open spaces for the lacing tie. On one side of the hemstitching the fabric is a little wider and rests on the shoulders; the narrower side forms a gentle ruffle on top.

PETER PAN COLLAR

We've employed several techniques to create the unique and stylish result you see here. The vertical hemstitching is worked as the weaving proceeds; it creates a space for a lacing tie inserted after weaving to shape the neck. Little crocheted beads embellish the ends of the tie. In addition, narrow lines of slightly felted merino wool add a little ruffle to the edges. This is the ideal project for those who never want to grow up.

Designed and woven by Stephanie Flynn Sokolov

Finished size: 6¾" (17 cm) wide and 21" (53.5 cm) long, plus ¼" (6 mm) of fringe at each end.

Structure: Plain weave with lengthwise hemstitching.

Equipment: 10" (25.5 cm) wide, 10-dent rigid heddle reed; one stick shuttle, two tapestry needles; size U.S. 7 (1.65 mm) steel crochet hook; Incredible Rope Machine.

Yarn: *Habu Tsumugi Silk A-1* (100% silk at 4,235 yd/lb [3,872 m/453 g]) in #40 green (warp and weft): 225 yd (1 ball at 450 yd [411 m]/50 g).

Malabrigo Lace (100% ultrafine merino at 4,297 yd/lb [3929 m/453 g]) in #158 Cognac (warp only): 12 yd (1 skein at 470 yd [429 m]/50 g).

Warp length: 52" (132 cm), which includes 24" (61 cm) for loom waste and very short fringe at each end.

Total warp ends: 98 (90 ends of Tsumugi Silk and 8 ends of Malabrigo Lace).

Width in reed: 10" (25.5 cm).

Ends per inch: 10.

Picks per inch: 10.

Yarn Wrapping

This yarn wrapping is shown actual size to assist you in making substitutions. Just place the yarn you want to use on top of the yarn chart to see if the yarn is the same size. Substituting a yarn with similar fiber content will be most successful.

Top to bottom:

➤ Habu Tsumugi Silk A-1 in #40 green.
➤ Malabrigo Lace in #158 Cognac.

Warping

Use the direct peg method (page 146) to thread 51 slots total as follows:

4 slots with Tsumugi Silk

2 slots with Malabrigo Lace

16 slots with Tsumugi Silk

Leave 2 slots empty

21 slots with Tsumugi Silk (the ruffle on this side is longer than on the other side)

2 slots with Malabrigo Lace

4 slots of Tsumugi Silk

Weaving

Wind Tsumugi Silk on the stick shuttle.

Allow sufficient length in your front tie-on for a 2" (5 cm) fringe.

Leaving a tail four times the weaving width for hemstitching, weave 6 picks.

making a crocheted Bead

Leaving a 5" (12.5 cm) tail, chain 3 and join with a slip stitch to form a ring.

Work 4 single crochet (sc) in center of ring.

Work 1 sc in each of the 4 sc.

*Work 2 sc in next sc, 1 sc in next sc; rep from * 2 more times—7 sc total.

Work 1 sc in each of the 7 sc.

Stuff beginning tail into the bead, then [insert hook into stitch, yarn over, pull through stitch, insert hook into next stitch, yarn over, pull through stitch, yarn over, pull through all loops on the hook] five times.

Fasten off and thread finishing tail through bead.

▲ *Off loom, before washing.*

Use the tail to hemstitch (see page 153) over 2 warp ends and 2 weft picks.

Weave at 10 ppi for 28" (71 cm), working 2 rows of vertical hemstitching along the length of the scarf to form the "fold line" when the collar is removed from the loom. Work vertical ladder hemstitching (see box at right) over 2 warps and 3 wefts, taking care to align the lines of hemstitching so that the gathering rope can easily thread through the spaces. For efficiency, stop weaving every few inches and work the vertical hemstitching up to the fell of the cloth.

Finishing

Remove the fabric from the loom, untying the knots in front.

Handwash in hot water, rubbing the Malabrigo Lace stripes until they felt.

Place the scarf in the dryer on low heat for 15 minutes or until dry, checking it often.

Steam-press on medium heat, being careful to not crush the ripples created by the felted Malabrigo.

Straighten the fringe and press hard with an iron.

Use a rotary cutter and a ruler to trim the fringe evenly at ¼" (6 mm).

To make the rope to cinch the scarf, use the Incredible Rope Machine to twist a 46" (117 cm) long rope made of three strands of Tsumugi Silk.

Embellish each end of the rope with small crocheted beads as described on page 122.

Weave the rope over and under the ladder of threads created by the hemstitching.

vertical Ladder Hemstitching

Vertical hemstitching requires an unthreaded space in the heddle. In this case, we left a slot, hole, slot, hole, and slot unthreaded to create an open space in the woven web where only weft floats appear.

To begin, measure two lengths of warp yarn four times the length of your weaving and thread each on a separate tapestry needle. (If your weaving is very long, you may prefer to use several shorter lengths, adding new ones as necessary.)

Weave several inches as usual.

Step 1. Working individually with one needle on each side of the gap, insert the needle under 3 weft picks and 2 warp ends, just as you would for regular hemstitching, and bring the needle to the surface and pull the yarn through.

Step 2. Make a loop with the working end of yarn, then insert the needle vertically under the same 3 weft picks, catching the loop. Pull tight to gather the weft threads.

Repeat Steps 1 and 2, working in short sections on each side of the gap as you weave the cloth.

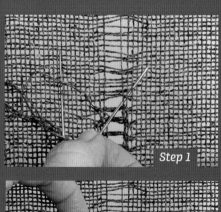
Step 1

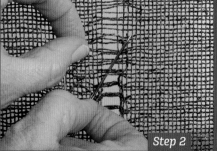
Step 2

The fine wool yarn used here is sett at 12 epi and woven at 24 ppi for a fairly open weave. Even though we warped the loom for the full 10" (25.5 cm) width of the reed, the felting process results in a scarf that's only 4½" (11.5 cm) wide— that's 65% shrinkage!

FELT RESIST BANANAGRAM SCARF

This scarf's unique look is created by making a felt resist with Bananagram tiles (other small plastic tiles could be used as well), then controlling the finishing of the fabric to create permanent three-dimensional shapes. The technique is simple: after weaving, tiles are secured in the fabric with small rubber bands. The fabric is then heavily fulled or felted, leaving permanent shapes in the fabric in a design created by where it was allowed to felt and where it wasn't.

Designed and woven by Stephanie Flynn Sokolov

Finished size: 4½" (11.5 cm) wide and 53" (134.5 cm) long.

Structure: Plain weave with shaped, resist felting.

Equipment: 10" (25.5 cm) wide, 12-dent rigid heddle reed; one stick shuttle; 73 Bananagram tiles; 73 small rubber bands.

Yarn: *Jojoland Harmony* (100% merino wool at 8,000 yd/lb [7,315 m/453 g]) in #HC06 red/green/blue mix (warp and weft): 1,060 yd total; 350 yd for warp and 600 yd for weft (2 balls at 880 yd [804 m]/50 g).

Warp length: 104" (264 cm), which allows for 24" (61 cm) of loom waste.

Total warp ends: 120.

Width in reed: 10" (25.5 cm).

Ends per inch: 12.

Picks per inch: 24.

Yarn Wrapping

This yarn wrapping is shown actual size to assist you in making substitutions. Just place the yarn you want to use on top of the yarn chart to see if the yarn is the same size. Substituting a yarn with similar fiber content will be most successful.

➤ Jojoland Harmony in #HC06 red/green/ blue mix.

Warping

Use the direct peg method (page 146).

Weaving

Wind Harmony on the stick shuttle.

Leaving a tail four times the weaving width for hemstitching, weave 3 picks.

Beat these picks firmly to compact them together, then use the tail to hemstitch (see page 153) over 3 warp ends and 3 weft picks.

Weave for as long as your warp will allow.

Hemstitch over 3 warps and 3 wefts.

Finishing

Remove the fabric from the loom.

Creating the Resist

Lay the fabric flat. Beginning about 1" (2.5 cm) from one end of the scarf, secure the tiles in a series of rows, leaving about 2½" (6.5 cm) between rows. For the first row, position three tiles evenly spaced across the width. Place each tile underneath the fabric, pushing it into the fabric and securing it in place from above the fabric with a small rubber band. For the second row, secure two tiles evenly between the tiles in the first row. Repeat in this manner for the length of the scarf. To help with even spacing along the length of the scarf, work from both ends and finish in the middle.

Felting

Place the scarf in a lingerie bag and wash on the delicate cycle in the washing machine with cold water and mild detergent. If you're not sure of the delicate setting on your washing machine or are terrified of throwing it all in the machine, leave the scarf in a lingerie bag and wash it by hand in the sink with vigorous agitation. Check the scarf often to see how the felting is going. If it looks sufficiently felted, remove it from the machine and rinse it in lukewarm water. If the scarf needs further felting, place it in the lingerie bag in the dryer on medium heat and check it often.

When the scarf is almost dry, remove it from the bag and shape and reposition any tiles that have shifted. Steam-press them into place, using a pressing cloth to crisp up the edges of the fabric that is stretched over the tiles and hasn't felted.

Use small scissors to cut the rubber bands and gently ease the tiles out of the fabric. Trim the felted fringe to ⅛" (3 mm).

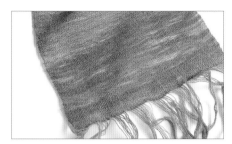

▲ Fabric off loom, before washing.

▲ We used the plastic tiles from the Bananagram game and small rubber bands.

▲ Place the tile under the fabric and hold it in place, slipping the rubber band over it to secure it in the fabric.

▲ Fabric ready for washing.

Cashmere yarn used for the weft of this scarf was raveled from a thrift-store find. Should your recycled yarn be super fine, you could double it in the weft to yield the desired hand. As is always our advice when you work with somewhat unknown materials: sample first.

RECYCLED SWEATER SCARF

You can participate in the popular use of re-purposed or recycled materials in your next scarf. For this soft and simple piece, a black cashmere sweater was raveled and used for the weft yarn, juxtaposed against a spaced-dyed superwash wool in the warp. The result is pleasing warpwise color variation along the length of the scarf. You can find recycled garments at your local thrift shop. Look for labels with yummy fiber content, such as the cashmere used for this scarf—luxury yarn at a bargain price.

Designed and woven by Betty Paepke

Finished size: 7" (18 cm) wide and 60" (152.5 cm) long, with 6" (15 cm) twisted fringe at each end.

Structure: Plain weave with spaced warps.

Equipment: 10" (25.5 cm) wide, 12-dent rigid heddle reed; one stick shuttle; fringe twister (optional).

Yarn: *Koigu Premium Merino KPPPM* (100% washable merino wool at 1,554 yd/lb [1,420 m/453 g] in #0325 dark gray/light gray/olive green mix (warp only): 210 yd (2 skeins at 170 yd [155 m]/50 g).

Yarn recovered from a cashmere sweater (our yarn yielded 7,500 yd/lb [6,858 m/453 g]) in black: 325 yd.

Warp length: 90" (229 cm), which allows 24" (61 cm) for loom waste and includes 12" (30.5 cm) fringe—6" (15 cm) fringe at each end.

Total warp ends: 84.

Width in reed: 9½" (24 cm).

Ends per inch: 12.

Picks per inch: 16.

Yarn Wrapping

This yarn wrapping is shown actual size to assist you in making substitutions. Just place the yarn you want to use on top of the yarn chart to see if the yarn is the same size. Substituting a yarn with similar fiber content will be most successful.

Top to bottom:

➤ Koigu Premium Merino KPPPM in #0325 dark gray/ light gray/olive green mix.

➤ 2-ply cashmere from a recycled black cashmere sweater.

Raveling the Sweater

In general, manufactured sweaters are sewn together with a chain stitch, which can be easily pulled apart. To begin deconstructing the sweater, open the sleeve seam and pull at the stitches holding the sweater together.

Next, remove the sleeves from the body of the sweater, then remove the ribbing at the neck edge.

Snip and pull on a bottom or top thread to release a raveling thread. Wind the yarn in to a ball as you go.

Use a swift to transform the balls into skeins.

Wash the skeins to remove the kinks (you may need to weight the skeins lightly to straighten the kinks).

▲ *Begin with a sweater you no longer wear or get one from a thrift store.*

▲ *Pull on the yarn to ravel the sweater.*

Warping

Using the direct peg method (page 146), follow the warping plan below.

Warping Plan

		Repeat 3 times			Total
Koigu	24		12	24	84
Empty*		8		8	

*leave 8 spaces (4 slots) empty.

Weaving

Wind the recovered yarn onto the stick shuttle.

Allow sufficient length in your front tie on for 8" (20 cm) of fringe and leaving a tail four times the weaving width for hemstitching, weave several picks.

Use the tail to hemstitch (see page 153) over 2 warp ends and 2 weft picks.

Weave at 16 ppi for 60" (152.5 cm), advancing the warp often to help maintain an even beat.

Hemstitch over 2 warps and 2 wefts.

Finishing

Remove the fabric from the loom, untying the knots in front to allow for fringe.

Using a fringe twister, if desired, make 6" (15 cm) twisted fringe (see page 25) from two groups of two warp ends each, securing the ends with an overhand knot about 2" (5 cm) from the end of each group.

Handwash in hot, soapy water (use rubber gloves if necessary). Rinse.

Place the scarf and a bath towel (or two) in the dryer set on medium heat to further full the fabric, checking progress often to prevent felting the fabric.

Trim the fringe to 6" (15 cm).

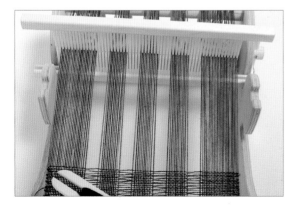

▲ The scarf on the loom. Spaced warps enhance both the look and drape of the scarf.

▲ The fabric removed from the loom before washing. Be sure to twist the fringe before washing.

Just a 3" (7.5 cm) wide warp is required for this fringy accessory. While we've made a neck adornment, the techniques could be used for other applications as well.

FRINGY COLLAR

With this piece, we take the concept of the scarf and push it to the extreme to fashion a fringy neck adornment. We used a commercial knit fabric, but this idea lends itself well to recycling old T-shirts or sweatpants as well. The key to this look is using a knit fabric (ideally one that includes spandex) that will curl when cut.

Designed and woven by Jane Patrick

Finished size: 7" (18 cm) wide (including fringe) and 16" (40.5 cm) long.

Structure: Plain weave with Ghiordes knots and inlaid fringe.

Equipment: 10" (25.5 cm) wide 10-dent rigid heddle reed; stick shuttle; rotary cutter; healing mat; T-square; small pair of pliers; one ¼" (6 mm) snap.

Yarn: *UKI 5/2 pearl cotton* (100% cotton at 2,100 yd/lb [1,920 m/453 g]) in #114 Orange (warp and background weft):

120 yd (1 tube at 788 yd [721 m]/6 oz).

Fabric strips for weft pile (82% nylon, 18% spandex at 60" [152.5 cm] wide) in gray (weft only): 464 strips, each cut to 9" (23 cm) long and ½" (1.3 cm) wide (about 1 yd [1 m] of 60" [152.5 cm] knit fabric).

Warp length: 44" (112 cm), which includes 24" (61 cm) for loom waste.

Total warp ends: 30.

Width in reed: 3" (7.5 cm).

Ends per inch: 10.

Picks per inch: 36 in background areas.

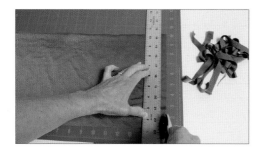

▲ *Use a healing mat, T-square, and rotary cutter to cut the fabric into ½" (1.3 cm) wide strips.*

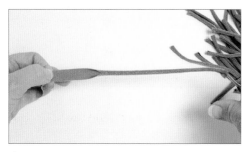

▲ *Pull on the strips to force them to curl.*

Yarn Wrapping

This yarn wrapping is shown actual size to assist you in making substitutions. Just place the yarn you want to use on top of the yarn chart to see if the yarn is the same size. Substituting a yarn with similar fiber content will be most successful.

Top to bottom:

➤ UKI 5/2 pearl cotton in #114 Orange.
➤ Fabric strips for weft pile in gray.

Preparing the Fabric Strips

Cut off the selvedges before cutting the strips. Cut along the grain of the fabric so that the long edges will curl (test the fabric first by cutting a strip in one direction or the other to see which piece will curl when pulled).

Cut the fabric into four 9" (23 cm) strips (cut two layers at once to speed the cutting).

Use a healing mat, T-square, and rotary cutter to cut these strips into smaller strips that are ½" (1.3 cm) wide each. (This work can be tiring, so you might want to break up the cutting into several sessions.)

Curl the strips by grabbing one end with a pair of pliers and pulling the other end with your other hand. When pulled, the strips will measure about 11" (28 cm) each.

Warping

Use the direct peg method (page 146).

Weaving

Wind 5/2 Pearl Cotton on stick shuttle.

Leaving a tail four times the weaving width for hemstitching, weave 3 picks.

Use the tail to hemstitch (see page 153) over 2 warp ends and 3 weft picks.

Weave 1½" (3.8 cm) for hem.

Beginning at the right edge, weave pile pattern as follows:

Step 1. With shed closed, skip the first 2 warp ends, then make a sideways Ghiordes knot around the next 2 warp ends by folding the fabric strip in half, placing the fold under the 2 warps (warps 3 and 4) from right to left, bringing the fold up to the surface, placing the ends through the loop and pulling tight to secure. You'll make just one sideways Ghiordes knot per row.

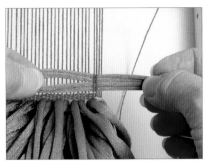

▲ *Pull the folded fabric strip under 2 warp ends so that the loop is to the left.*

▲ *Bring the ends through the loop and pull tight to secure.*

▲ *Insert the strips as inlay (do not knot them), centered between each adjacent pair of warp ends.*

Step 2. Place heddle in down shed and work seven inlay strips (without knots) across the rest of the width. Begin by inserting a strip of fabric into the shed under the next 2 warps. Pull on the 2 ends to center the strip and pull down to the fell of the cloth. Insert the next strip under the next 2 raised warp threads, and so on across the warp. The left side of the last strip will hang out at the selvedge.

Step 3. Use a hand beater to press down gently on the row of inlays to compact them in place.

Step 4. Beginning with the shed down (the same shed as the row of knots), weave 6 picks with Pearl Cotton.

Repeat Steps 1–4 for a total of 58 rows of inlay and Ghiordes knots.

Weave 3 picks.

Hemstitch over 2 warp ends and 3 weft picks.

Finishing

Remove the fabric from the loom.

Use a steam iron and pressing cloth to lightly steam the back of the fabric to the best of your ability.

To shape and curve one edge of the collar, pull the two warp threads on the edge with the Ghiordes knots to cinch the edge about 1½" (3.8 cm) shorter than the other edge.

Trim the warp fringe to just ¼" (6 mm), then fold it under twice to make a double hem that measures ½" (1.3 cm). Handsew in place to secure.

Sew a snap on the top (shortest edge) as a closure.

◄ *Pull the warp threads along the edge that has the knotted strips to shape the collar.*

A light and airy scarf is created by using an energized weft that collapses to create a ripply surface.

METAMORPHOSIS

Much like the metamorphosis of a butterfly, a fabric can be transformed in a collapse weave that seems magical. For this scarf, an over-twisted crepe weft is the change agent—it alters an open weave in fine yarns into a rippled wonder. Because the yarn is treated with sizing to keep it from twisting during the weaving process, you can't see what's to come in the finishing process. But once the sizing is washed away, it's hard to believe it's the same scarf you took off the loom. This scarf is a favorite because it is easy to weave, but it results in a magical fabric at the end. The outcome far exceeds the effort.

Designed and woven by Stephanie Flynn Sokolov

Finished size: 5" (12.5 cm) wide and 53" (134.5 cm) long, plus 4" (10 cm) of fringe at each end.

Structure: Collapsed plain weave.

Equipment: 10" (25.5 cm) wide, 12-dent rigid heddle reed; one stick shuttle (or one slim boat shuttle, one bobbin, and a bobbin winder); tapestry needle.

Yarn: *Habu 2/17 Tsumugi Silk* (100% silk at 4,235 yd/ lb [3,872 m/453 g]) in Café (warp only): 325 yd (1 ball at 450 yd [411 m]/50 g).

Habu Wool Crepe (100% wool crepe at 15,040 yd/ lb [13,752 m/453 g]) in RW 3030 (weft only): 470 yd (1 cone at 940 yd [859 m]/1 oz). *Note: This yarn has been discontinued; substitute Habu N-89 (747 yd [672 m]/1 oz) in #32 Murasaki purple.*

Warp length: 97" (246 cm), which includes 24" (61 cm) for loom waste and 4" (10 cm) of fringe at each end.

Total warp ends: 120.

Width in reed: 10" (25.5 cm).

Ends per inch: 12.

Picks per inch: About 21.

Yarn Wrapping

This yarn wrapping is shown actual size to assist you in making substitutions. Just place the yarn you want to use on top of the yarn chart to see if the yarn is the same size. Substituting a yarn with similar fiber content will be most successful.

Top to bottom:

➤ Habu 2/17 Tsumugi Silk in Café.

➤ Habu Wool Crepe in RW 3030 Chocolate.

Weave at 21 ppi (measured off tension) until piece measures 71" (180 cm), or until you can't weave any further.

Hemstitch over 2 warps and 3 wefts.

Notes: *Because there are so many picks per inch, you can speed up the process by using a slim boat shuttle. It handles the somewhat wiry wool crepe yarn quite well by keeping the yarn under constant tension around the bobbin.*

When you wind bobbins, it helps to keep the crepe yarn under constant tension by running it through a couple of eye hooks on a winding station. Alternately, you could set up a little obstacle course for the crepe yarn with warping pegs to provide extra tension.

When you weave fine threads, it's a good idea to separate the layers around the cloth beam with paper. Use the paper for at least the first couple of revolutions around the cloth beam until the woven material starts to wrap around itself. Covering the apron cords on the cloth beam helps you avoid unevenness when weaving fine threads.

Warping

Use the direct peg method (page 146).

Because the warp yarn has a loose twist, it requires gentle handling to prevent untwisting. We advise handling it as little as possible when you tie onto the front apron rod, then tensioning the warp quite tightly.

Weaving

Wind Wool Crepe onto the shuttle. Allow sufficient length in your front tie-on for a 6" (15 cm) fringe.

Leaving a tail four times the weaving width for hemstitching, weave 3 picks.

Use the tail to hemstitch (see page 153) over 2 warp ends and 3 weft picks.

Finishing

Remove the fabric from the loom, untying the knots in the front tie-on to allow for fringe.

Working with 2 warp ends per group, work twisted fringe (see page 25) for about 6" (15 cm, though the exact length doesn't matter) at each end.

Handwash in warm water with a small amount of soap and vigorous agitation to remove the starch from the weft yarn, thereby "energizing" it. Doing so releases the over-twist in the yarn and causes the fabric to collapse.

Place the wet scarf in a lingerie bag in the dryer on low heat for 10 minutes. Check the progress and remove the scarf while still slightly damp.

Hang the scarf over a rod or lay it flat until fully dry.

Finish the ends by tying tight overhand knots on the twisted fringe bundles about 4" (10 cm) from the edge of the cloth. Use sharp scissors to clip just beyond the knots.

▲ *The scarf before washing and, therefore, before the weft "collapses" to pull in the weave widthwise.*

measuring your weaving

How do you keep track of how much you've woven? You can always unwind the weaving, but we don't recommend it because it can be difficult to re-establish the same tension.

Instead, cut a non-stretchy string yarn, such as cotton carpet warp or pearl cotton the target length of your weaving. Use a T-pin to secure one end of the string to the beginning of the weaving in the middle. As your weaving progresses, just roll up the measuring string with the cloth on the front beam—the loose bit of string will indicate the amount of warp you have left, and from that you can deduce the length you've woven.

The weaving of this scarf is straightforward plain weave. We love the many pattern-and-weave effects along the length, which add to the scarf's intriguing patterning. You could simplify the patterning by replacing just one of the motifs. If you love the look but don't want to dye, simply omit the discharge treatment for another knockout look.

STEAMPUNK SCARF

The cog motifs on this captivating piece of color-and-weave patterning are achieved by discharge dyeing—using bleach to purposefully remove some of the color on the woven fabric. For this technique, the weaving is completed and the fabric washed to full it before the discharge dyeing. For this piece, we used a bleach pen to remove the color within stenciled areas. The bleach is applied to an area of the fabric and allowed to dry, then the next section treated, and so on. The result is a fascinating pattern that truly makes each piece a one-of-a-kind masterpiece.

Designed and woven by Stephanie Flynn Sokolov

Finished size: 9" (23 cm) wide and 70" (178 cm) long, plus 8" (20.5 cm) of fringe at each end.

Structure: Plain weave.

Equipment: 10" (25.5 cm) wide, 12-dent rigid heddle reed; two stick shuttles; paper or plastic for stencil; protective work surface; tape; Clorox Bleach pen (use a new pen for this purpose because an old one might not be as effective).

Yarn: *Cotton Clouds Bambu 7* (100% bamboo at 2,100 yd/lb [1,920 m/453 g]) in #360 Onyx (warp and weft): 510 yd (1 cone at 525 yd [480 m]/100 g).

Gutermann Metallic Sewing Thread (100% polyester at 18,800 yd/lb [17,190 m/453 g]) in #036 Copper (warp and weft): 510 yd (1 spool at 547 yd [500 m]/14 g tube).

Giovanna Imperia Designs Japanese Metallics NS46 (polyester-nylon blend at 10,600 yd/lb [9,692 m/453 g]) in copper (warp and weft): 160 yd (1 cone at 550 yd [503 m]/8 oz).

Warp length: 94" (239 m), which includes 24" (61 cm) for loom waste and 8" (20.5 cm) of fringe at each end.

Total warp ends: 118.

Width in reed: 9¾" (25 cm).

Ends per inch: 12.

Picks per inch: 11 to 12.

Yarn Wrapping

This yarn wrapping is shown actual size to assist you in making substitutions. Just place the yarn you want to use on top of the yarn chart to see if the yarn is the same size. Substituting a yarn with similar fiber content will be most successful.

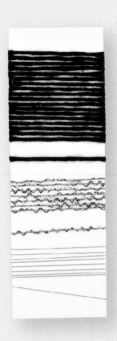

Top to bottom:

➤ Cotton Clouds Bambu 7 in #360 Onyx.

➤ Giovanna Imperia Designs Japanese Metallics NS46 in copper.

➤ Gutermann Metallic Sewing Thread in #036 Copper.

▲ *The scarf on the loom, before resist dyeing.*

Warping

Using the indirect method (see page 151) measure the warp yarns on a warping board, follow the warping plan at right.

Weaving

The entire scarf is woven in plain weave. There are 2 wefts: a strand of the metallic Gutermann thread and a strand of the Bambu 7 used together (referred to as "bamboo" in the weaving instructions) and a single strand of the Japanese metallic yarn (referred to as "metallic" in the weaving instructions) in the color-and-weave areas. When you wind the shuttle with the two yarns, use very little tension on the yarns so that they'll wind on at the same tension.

Allow sufficient length in your front tie-on for an 11" (28 cm) fringe.

Leaving a tail four times the weaving width for hemstitching, weave 2 picks of bamboo.

Use the tail to hemstitch (see page 153) over 2 warp ends and 2 weft picks.

Weave 6" (15 cm) with bamboo.

Warping Plan

			Repeat 2 times			Repeat 9 times			Repeat 12 times			Repeat 3 times			
G*	2		1			1						1		2	18
g									1						12
b		2		1	14		2	8		1	14		6		88
Total Ends															**118**

G=doubled Japanese Metallics NS46; g= single end of Japanese Metallics NS46;
b=bamboo with metallic Gutermann thread; *= working ends (some ends are doubled).

Alternate 1 pick each of bamboo and metallic until there are a total of 11 picks of metallic.

Weave 9" (23 cm) with bamboo.

Alternate 1 pick of metallic and 6 picks of bamboo until there are a total of 5 stripes of metallic.

Weave 12" (30.5 cm) with bamboo.

Using the metallic yarn doubled, alternate 1 pick of metallic and 2 picks of bamboo until there is a total of 9 metallic stripes.

Weave 9" (23 cm) with bamboo.

Alternate 1 pick each of metallic and bamboo until there are a total of 3 metallic stripes, then weave 5 picks of bamboo.

Repeat this sequence once more, then end by alternating 1 pick of metallic and 1 pick of bamboo three times.

Weave 9" (23 cm) with bamboo.

Alternate 1 pick of metallic and 6 picks of bamboo until there are 5 metallic stripes.

Weave 12" (30.5 cm) with bamboo.

Alternate 1 pick each of metallic and bamboo until there are a total of 15 metallic stripes.

Weave 7" (18 cm) with bamboo.

Alternate 1 pick of metallic and 3 picks of bamboo until there are a total of 3 metallic stripes.

Weave 1" (2.5 cm) with bamboo.

With bamboo, hemstitch over 2 warps and 2 wefts.

Finishing

Remove the fabric from the loom, untying the knots in the front tie-on to allow for fringe.

Handwash in warm water.

Place in the dryer on low heat until mostly dry.

Remove from dryer and hang until completely dry.

creating edge loops

A happy result of the finishing process is that the bamboo shrinks more than the metallic thread, which creates loops of gold along the edges. Simply pull the loops to various lengths away from the selvedge for an irregular look.

If desired, you can eliminate loops of metallic thread along the length of the warp by pulling on the threads in the fringe until the loops disappear.

Discharge Dyeing

Note: *If you use different materials or products, we suggest you try out the bleach on a sample swatch of the fabric before working on your scarf.*

Step 1. Cut stencils from heavy plastic (we used protective covers from fabric sample books). We purchased these images from a website (see sidebar on page 145), but you could make your own.

Step 2. Beginning at one end and working on a protected surface (we secured plastic wrap over a cutting board by taping it to the back of the board), position the stencils over the scarf as desired—use as many or as few as you like. Tape the stencil in place.

Step 3. Wearing old clothes or an apron to prevent mishaps, shake the bleach pen thoroughly. Squirt a bit of bleach onto a scrap fabric or a paper towel to ensure that it's thoroughly mixed into a thick liquid that won't leak into unwanted areas.

Step 4. Start in the center of an open area and work toward the edges to control the bleach and keep the edges nice and crisp. When the bleach has discharged enough of the color so you can clearly see the pattern, remove the stencil and touch up the design as necessary.

Step 5. Allow the bleach to dry, then proceed to the next section, repeating the process along the length of the scarf.

Let the scarf sit for 20 minutes to ensure that the bleach is completely dry.

Handwash in warm water and rinse well.

Place the scarf in the dryer for 20 minutes or until almost dry, remove from the dryer, and hang to dry.

▲ *Working in sections, position the stencils as desired on top of the woven fabric.*

▲ *Apply bleach to the stencil, starting in the center and working toward the edges.*

Steam-press under a pressing cloth.

Trim fringe to 8" (20.5 cm).

Variation

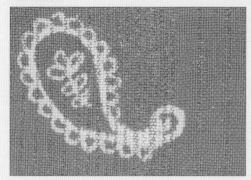

➤ This variation was inspired by paisley fabric. It's a simple design that would make a great beginning pattern. We used Bambu 7 in Fuchsia for this sample, which bleaches bright white for a crisp design.

Designed by Stephanie Flynn Sokolov

making stencils

We purchased the images used for this scarf from www.123rf.com, image #12397620. From these printed images we traced the pattern onto heavyweight clear plastic with a Sharpie. We then cut along the lines using an X-Acto knife to make the stencil. If you choose a motif with an open pattern like this, you may find that you need to temporarily tape sections together to prevent the stencil from moving around as you work.

APPENDIX

Direct, Single-Peg Warping Method

This method offers a fast and easy way to start weaving in a jiffy. It's particularly useful when you have only one warp yarn or when your warp will be threaded in pairs or even numbers.

Step 1. Clamp the back of the loom to the top of a table **(photo 1)**.

Step 2. Determine the length of your warp. Place the peg that distance away from the back apron rod (the peg will be closest to the front of the loom).

Step 3. Place the yarn source on the floor under the back beam of the loom.

Step 4. Place the heddle in the neutral position.

Step 5. Determine the width of the weaving. To center the weaving in the heddle, subtract the width of the weaving from the width of the heddle and divide that number by two. Doing so gives you the distance from the edge of the heddle where you need to start threading **(photo 2)**.

Step 6. Bring the apron rod up and over the back beam. Tie the warp end to the apron rod in line with one edge of the weaving width **(photo 3)**.

Step 7. Insert the heddle hook from the front side to the back, grab the warp yarn, and draw it through the slot **(photo 4)**.

▶ Photo 1. Clamp the back of the loom to the top of a table.

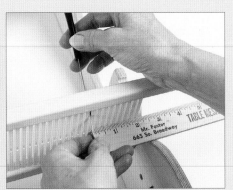

▶ Photo 2. Determine the edge of the weaving based on the difference between the width of the heddle and the width of the weaving.

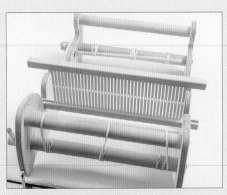

▶ Photo 3. Tie the warp end to the apron rod in line with one edge of the weaving width.

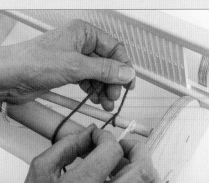

▶ Photo 4. Grab the warp yarn with the heddle hook and draw it through the slot.

▶ *Photo 5.* Place the loop around the warping peg.

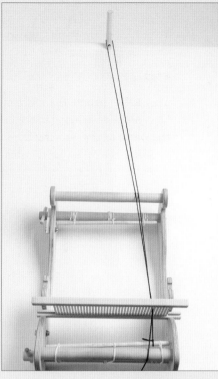

▶ *Photo 6.* Grab the next loop from under the apron bar.

▶ *Photo 7.* Grab the next loop from over the apron bar.

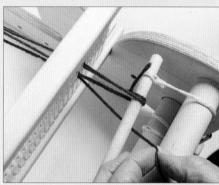

▶ *Photo 8.* To change colors, tie off the old color on the apron rod, then tie on the new color.

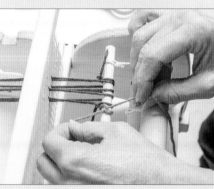

▶ *Photo 9.* To alternate two ends of a color, sley every other slot (shown), then fill in the spaces with the second color.

Step 8. Place this loop around the warping peg. There will be 2 warp ends through the slot **(photo 5)**.

Note: *The warp yarn alternates between going over the back apron bar and going under it* **(photos 6 and 7)**. *This is as it should be.*

Note: *To change colors, simply tie off one yarn, then tie on the new color* **(photo 8)**.

Note: *If you're alternating 2 ends of a color, you can sley every other slot, then fill in the spaces with the second color* **(photo 9)**.

► **Photo 10.** Draw loops through the slots and around the warping peg for the total number of warp ends.

► **Photo 11.** Cut the yarn and tie the end onto the apron rod.

► **Photo 12.** Cut the loops that were around the warping peg.

► **Photo 13.** Tie the ends in a loose overhand knot.

► **Photo 14.** Wind the warp onto the back warp beam.

► Photo 15. As you wind the warp onto the back warp beam, place heavy paper between the layers.

► Photo 16. Continue winding until the knot approaches the front of the heddle.

► Photo 17. Untie a section of the knot, take one warp end out of a slot, and thread it in the adjacent hole.

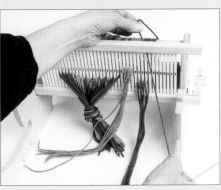

► Photo 18. Check to make sure that there is one warp end through each slot and one end through each hole across the weaving width.

Step 9. Continue to draw loops through the slots and around the warping peg for the desired total number of warp ends **(photo 10)**.

Step 10. Cut the yarn and tie the end onto the apron rod **(photo 11)**.

Step 11. Remove the loops of warp from the warping peg, cut the ends of the loops **(photo 12)**, and tie them in a loose overhand knot **(photo 13)**.

Step 12. Wind the warp onto the back warp beam **(photo 14)** between layers of heavy paper or corrugated cardboard **(photo 15)**. Continue winding on until the knot approaches the front of the heddle **(photo 16)**.

Step 13. Untie the overhand knot and separate out a 2" (5 cm) section. Working at the front of the loom, take 1 warp end out of a slot and thread it in the adjacent hole **(photo 17)**. It usually doesn't matter if you go to the right or left; just be consistent across the warp.

Step 14. When all of the slots and holes have been threaded, check to make sure that there is 1 warp end through each slot and 1 warp end through each hole across the weaving width **(photo 18)**.

Step 15. To tie the warp onto the front apron rod in a surgeon's knot, pull a 1" (2.5 cm) bundle of warp ends over the top of the apron rod, divide it in half **(photo 19)**, then tie the 2 ends on top of the bundle using a surgeon's knot (left over right and left over right again) **(photo 20)**, tightening the knot against the apron rod **(photo 21)**. Repeat across the entire warp.

Step 16. Adjust each knot as necessary until the warp tension is even across the entire width **(photo 22)**, then tie the ends in bows to secure the bundles **(photo 23)**.

You are now ready to weave.

▶ Photo 19. Pull a 1" (2.5 cm) bundle over the top of the apron rod and divide it in half.

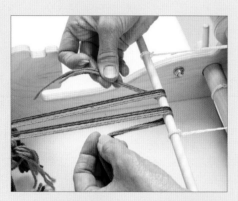

▶ Photo 20. Tie the two ends on top of the bundle, left over right, left over right.

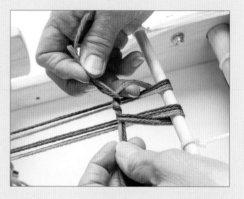

▶ Photo 21. Tighten the knot against the apron rod.

▶ Photo 22. Adjust each knot until you feel even tension across the entire warp width.

▶ Photo 23. Tie the ends into bows to secure the bundles.

Measuring a Warp Using a Warping Board

When your warp plan calls for an occasional single end of a yarn, odd numbers, a randomly sleyed pattern, or a mixed warp, you can simplify the threading process if you measure the warp first on a warping board.

Step 1. Determine the length of your warp. An easy way to figure out which pegs to use on the warping board for the warp length required is to measure a guide string the length of your warp, then wind it around the pegs to give you the length that you need.

Step 2. Tie the warp to the beginning peg and wind around the pegs as needed **(photo 1)**. When you get to the end make a figure eight around the last two pegs **(photo 2)**. The figure-eight shape is called the cross. The cross is your friend and will keep your threads in order so that you can easily manage them as you thread the heddle.

Step 3. Wind back to the beginning following the same path as before **(photo 3)**. When you return to your starting point you'll have measured 2 warp threads.

Note: *To change yarn colors, simply tie off one yarn and tie on the next* **(photo 4)**.

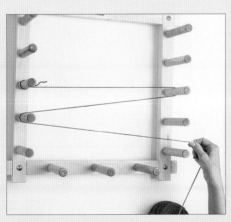

▶ Photo 1. Tie the warp to the beginning peg and wind around pegs as necessary for your warp length.

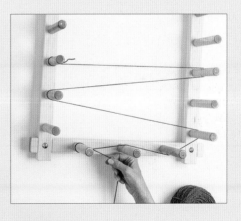

▶ Photo 2. Wrap a figure eight around the last two pegs.

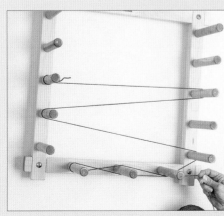

▶ Photo 3. Wind back to the beginning, following the same path.

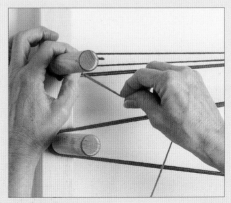

▶ Photo 4. To change yarn colors, tie off the old color and tie on the new.

Note: *When alternating colors appear in the warp, you can speed the measuring process by measuring the two colors together* **(photo 5)**.

Step 4. When you're back at the beginning peg, count the number of threads on one half of the cross **(photo 6)**, then multiply by two for the total number of ends measured.

Step 5. Before you remove the warp from the warping board, tie each side of the cross as well as the center of the cross with a contrasting color yarn to secure the warps at these points **(photo 7)**.

Step 6. For long warps, fasten choke ties along the length of the warp about 2 yards (1.8 m) apart to keep the warp chain orderly **(photo 8)**.

Step 7. Remove the warp from the warping board, cut the loops at the end opposite the cross **(photo 9)**, and tie them in an overhand knot.

You'll then take the measured warp to the loom and tie onto the front beam. Hold the cross in your hand and cut the end loop of the cross. The ends of the cross will stack up Lincoln Log–fashion.

► *Photo 5. If two colors will be alternated in the warp, hold two colors together when you wind.*

► *Photo 6. Count the ends on one half of the cross, then multiply by two for the total number of ends measured.*

► *Photo 7. Tie each side of the cross, as well as the center of the cross, before you remove the warp from the warping board.*

► *Photo 9. Cut the loops at the end opposite the cross.*

► *Photo 8. Fasten choke ties at intervals along the length of the warp to prevent tangles.*

▶ *Photo 1. Insert the needle diagonally from right to left under 3 warp ends and 3 weft picks, then up to the surface of the weaving.*

▶ *Photo 2. Insert the needle along the bottom edge under the 3 warp ends in this group and over the working yarn to encircle this group.*

▶ *Photo 3. Pull tight.*

▶ *Photo 4. Continue in this manner, inserting the needle under the next 3 warp ends and 3 weft picks.*

Hemstitching

Hemstitching is a great way to begin and end a scarf project. The hemstitch is known as a "weft protector" because it "protects" the weft from raveling. Hemstitching is easy to do under tension on the loom. The worst part about hemstitching is having to stop to do it when what you really want to do is to start weaving. On the other hand, the lovely result of hemstitching is that the ends of your weaving are secured when you remove it from the loom. Hemstitching also gives your scarf a tidy finish.

These instructions are written for those who work from right to left, but if you're left-handed, you may find it more comfortable to work from left to right.

The hemstitch is a two-part stitch; once you have the hang of it, hemstitching progresses smoothly.

Step 1. Leave a tail on the right side of your weaving about four times the width of your weaving.

Step 2. Weave 3 to 5 picks.

Step 3. Thread a tapestry needle with the tail of the yarn.

Step 4. Beginning at the right selvedge, insert the needle diagonally from right to left under 3 warp ends and 3 weft picks (or your desired number), and bring the needle to the surface **(photo 1)**.

Step 5. Insert the needle horizontally along the bottom edge under the 3 warp ends in this group and over the working yarn, encircling this group **(photo 2)**.

Step 6. Pull tight **(photo 3)**.

Repeat from Step 4 **(photo 4)** across the width of the weaving.

When you reach the left edge, sew the end in along the hemstitching or weave an inch or so into your woven web.

Your use of hemstitching can vary widely. You can use different-sized groupings, such as over 4 warps and up 2 wefts, depending on your yarn size as well as the look you desire. You can also use hemstitching as a design accent in the woven fabric.

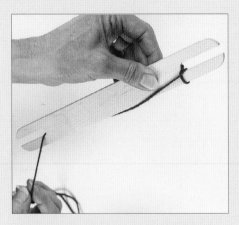

▲ *Photo 1. Bring the yarn up from the slot, across the top of the shuttle to the other end under the shuttle, and up through the slot.*

▲ *Photo 2. Bring the yarn across the top of the shuttle, then under the shuttle, and up through the slot to complete a figure-eight path.*

Winding a Shuttle

We like to wind the weft yarn in a figure eight along the edge of the stick shuttle. This technique allows more yarn to be loaded on the shuttle. It also lets the shuttle glide through the shed more readily, making weaving more efficient.

Step 1. Begin by wrapping the yarn once around one end of the shuttle.

Step 2. Bring the yarn up from the slot, across the top of the shuttle to the other end of the shuttle, under the shuttle, then up through the slot **(photo 1)**.

Step 3. Return to the end where you began, traveling across the top of the shuttle, then bringing the yarn up through the slot. If you think "up from the bottom, up from the bottom," you'll be winding in a figure-eight path **(photo 2)**.

Wind as much yarn on the shuttle as feels comfortable in your hand and allows the shuttle to slide easily through the shed. With this method, you can also wind the other side of the shuttle, thus doubling the shuttle's capacity.

How Much Yarn Do I Have?

Using stash yarn for projects can be tricky if you don't know how much yarn you have. You can always take your chances by eyeballing the yarn and guessing at the quantity. However, if you want to know for sure, you can use a McMorran Yarn Balance (or the Yarn to Yards Balance available from Eugene Textile Center). This simple tool weighs a length of yarn and lets you calculate the yardage per pound of the yarn. You can then weigh your yarn on a scale (such as the cooking scale shown here) to determine how many yards you have.

Here's how it works:

► **Photo 1.** Cut the yarn little by little until the arm is balanced.

► **Photo 2.** The arm will be horizontal when it is balanced.

► **Photo 3.** Measure the length of the balanced yarn.

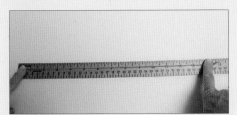

► **Photo 4.** Weigh the yarn to determine the total weight that you have.

Step 1. Balance the pin of the balance arm in the slots on the sides of the balance.

Step 2. Place a length of yarn in the notch of the arm.

Step 3. Cut the yarn little by little **(photo 1)** until the arm is balanced **(photo 2)**.

Step 4. Measure this length of yarn on a ruler **(photo 3)**.

Multiply this length by 100 to get the total yards per pound.

Step 5. Weigh the ball of yarn on a scale to find out the total weight of the yarn you have **(photo 4)**.

Step 6. To know if you have enough yarn, you'll need to do a little math.

In this example, our yarn measured 15" (38 cm) in length. We multiplied 15 by 100 to determine that there are 1,500 yards per pound of this yarn. We then weighed the ball of yarn and learned that it weighed 4 ounces. To find out how many yards were in these 4 ounces, we solved a simple equation:

$$\frac{1{,}500 \text{ yd}}{16 \text{ oz}} = \frac{X \text{ yd}}{4 \text{ oz}}$$

First multiply $4 \times 1{,}500 = 6{,}000$.

Then, divide this number by 16 to give the total amount of yarn: $6{,}000 \div 16 = 375$ yd.

GLOSSARY

apron rods. The bars connected to both the cloth beam and warp beam with apron cords to which the warp is tied.

balanced weave. Fabric in which the number of warp ends per inch is the same as the number of weft ends per inch.

beat. To push the weft threads into place with the rigid heddle reed.

collapse weave. Fabric that results in the movement of threads after the fabric is removed from the loom. There are two main methods used to achieve this effect: using high-twist yarns or yarns with different twist directions or weave structure.

cross. The figure eight made at one end of the warp when measuring. It keeps the warp ends in order and helps prevent tangles.

dent. Refers to both the slots and holes in the rigid heddle reed, i.e., 5-dent reed means that there are 5 warp threads per inch.

direct-peg warping. A method of warping the loom in which the warp is measured around a single peg and threaded through the reed in the same step.

end. One warp yarn (or thread).

epi (ends per inch). The number of warp threads in one inch.

fell line. The place on the loom where unwoven warp and web (or woven cloth) meet.

felting. The irreversible process of binding fibers (usually wool) together.

fiber. The substance, such as wool, from which yarn is spun.

finishing. The final process in making a woven fabric. After the fabric is removed from the loom, it needs to be washed, dried, or ironed or a combination of these.

floats. Any time a warp or weft yarn travels over more than one thread. Used to create weave patterns.

fulling. The finishing process given to a fabric after it is removed from the loom that causes the yarn to bloom and stabilizes the weave. Washing, machine drying, and heavy steam pressing are all used singly or together to full a fabric to the desired hand.

Ghiordes knot. A knot used to make pile. Also rya knot.

heddle. On a rigid heddle loom, the device that holds the warp, determines the sett, and beats the weft into place. Also rigid heddle reed.

hemstitching. A stitching technique used at the beginning or the end of weaving as a weft protector. May also be used to create pattern within a fabric.

leno. A finger technique that twists warp yarns to create spaces in the fabric.

loom. A frame that holds the warp taut for weaving.

loom waste. Any yarn that isn't woven at the beginning and end of a warp.

looped pile. Protruding loops made by looping weft yarn over a rod, with a tabby or plain-weave ground woven to lend structure.

novelty yarn. Generally a fancy, complex yarn that has unusual twists, irregularities, or fibers.

pick. One row of weaving. Also shot.

pick-and-pick. When two colors alternate in plain-weave rows (i.e., 1 row of white, 1 row of red, 1 row of white, 1 row of red).

pick-up. The technique of holding warp threads out of the way to create floats in weaving.

pick-up stick. A narrow stick used to pick up patterns. It can be turned on edge to form a shed. Also shed stick.

plain weave. The simplest of all weaves, an over, under, over, under interlacement.

plied yarn. A yarn that is composed of several single strands of yarn twisted together.

ppi (picks per inch). The number of weft rows, or picks, in one inch of weaving.

reed. See heddle.

rya knot. A knot used to make pile. Also Ghiordes knot.

selvedges. The edges of the cloth; also edge warp threads.

sett. Number of warp ends in 1 inch.

shed. The space between raised and lowered warp threads through which the shuttle passes during weaving.

shed stick. Narrow stick used to make a shed. Also pick-up stick.

shrinkage. The amount a fabric loses in the weaving and finishing process. Ten percent is generally figured for shrinkage during weaving. In the finishing process, depending on the method used, shrinkage could vary from 10% to 50%.

shuttle. The tool that holds yarn for weaving.

singles yarn. A yarn made of one strand; not a plied yarn.

sley. To thread the warp threads through the rigid heddle, generally with a threading hook.

Spanish lace. A finger-control technique to create pattern. It's created simply by weaving back and forth in one section for several rows and then moving on to the next section and weaving back and forth, and so on across the width of the weaving.

stick shuttle. Flat narrow stick with grooves on the ends used for weaving.

tabby. A plain-weave ground that binds pattern picks.

threading hook. A long flat metal hook with a handle used to thread the heddle.

warp. The set of threads held taut by a loom (noun); to put the warp threads on the loom (verb).

warp-emphasis: A fabric in which the warp dominates but doesn't completely cover the weft.

warping. The process of putting the warp on the loom.

warping board. A frame fitted with dowels that's used to measure the warp.

warping peg. A single peg that's clamped to a table and used to measure warp in the direct warping method.

weaving. Interlacing two sets of threads to make fabric. The warps are those threads held taut by a loom. The weft threads cross the warp.

web. On the loom, the warp that has been already woven.

weft. The threads that cross the warp.

weft-dominant. A fabric in which the weft is prominent but doesn't completely cover the warp.

weft-faced. Cloth in which only the weft shows.

weft protector. Any number of finishing processes that prevent the weft from raveling, including hemstitching, tied fringe, and twisted fringe.

yarn. Continuous fibers that have been spun or constructed.

yarn balance. A tool that weighs a length of yarn to determine the yardage per pound of a given yarn.

BIBLIOGRAPHY

Aimone, Katherine Duncan. *The Fiberarts Book of Wearable Art.* Asheville, North Carolina: Lark Books, 2002.

Baizerman, Suzanne, and Karen Searle. *Finishes in the Ethnic Tradition.* St. Paul, Minnesota: Dos Tejedoras, 1978.

Braddock, Sarah E., and Marie O'Mahony. *Techno Textiles.* New York: Thames & Hudson, 2001.

Davenport, Betty Linn. *Hands On Rigid Heddle Weaving.* Loveland, Colorado: Interweave, 1987.

———. *Textures and Patterns for the Rigid Heddle Loom.* Battle Ground, Washington: published by the author, distributed by Fine Fiber Press, 2008, revised edition.

Gipson, Liz. *Weaving Made Easy.* Loveland, Colorado: Interweave, 2008.

Hart, Rowena. *The Ashford Book of Rigid Heddle Weaving.* Ashburton, New Zealand: Ashford Handicrafts, 2002.

Howard, Sarah, and Elisabeth Kendrick. *Creative Weaving: Beautiful Fabrics with a Simple Loom.* Asheville, North Carolina: Lark Books, 2008.

Itten, Johannes. *The Elements of Color.* New York: Van Nostrand Reinhold, 1970.

Iwamura, Misao. *Plain Weaving: Try Creating Original Textiles Using Plain Weaving.* Tokyo: Bunko Publishing, 2002. English translation distributed in the United States by Habu Textiles.

Lamb, Sara. *Woven Treasures: One-of-Kind Bags with Folk Weaving Techniques.* Loveland, Colorado: Interweave, 2009.

Menz, Deb. *Color Works.* Loveland, Colorado: Interweave, 2004.

Patrick, Jane. *A Weaver's Idea Book.* Loveland, Colorado: Interweave, 2010.

Stockton, James. *Designer's Guide to Color.* San Francisco: Chronicle Books, 1984.

Sutton, Ann. *Colour-and-Weave Design Book: A Practical Reference Book.* England: Sterling Publishers, 1985.

———. *Ideas in Weaving.* Asheville, North Carolina: Lark Books, 1982.

Takekura, Masaaki, publisher. *Suke Suke.* Tokyo: Nuno Corporation, 1997.

Tidball, Harriet. *Surface Interest: Textiles of Today: Shuttle Craft Monograph Two.* Lansing, Michigan: The Shuttle Craft Guild, 1961.

———. *Undulating Weft Effects: Shuttle Craft Monograph Nine.* Freeland, Washington: HTH Publishers, 1963.

———. *Two-Harness Textiles: The Loom-Controlled Weaves: Shuttle Craft Monograph Twenty.* Santa Ana, California: HTH Publishers, 1967.

West, Virginia. *Finishing Touches for the Handweaver.* Loveland, Colorado: Interweave, 1988.

SOURCES

Alpaca with a Twist
950 S. White River Pkwy. W. Dr.
Indianapolis, IN 46221
alpacawithatwist.com

Be Sweet Inc.
7 Locust Ave.
Mill Valley, CA 94941
besweetproducts.com

Berroco
1 Tupperware Dr., Ste. 4
N. Smithfield, RI 02896
berroco.com

Brown Sheep Company
100662 County Rd. 16
Mitchell, NE 69357
brownsheep.com

Classic Elite Yarns
16 Esquire Rd., Unit 2
North Billerica, MA 01862
classiceliteyarns.com

Cotton Clouds
5176 S. 14th Ave.
Safford, AZ 85546
cottonclouds.com

Erdal Yarns
338 Northern Blvd., #5
Great Neck, NY 11021

Giovanna Imperia Designs
208 Emerson
Houston, TX 77006
giovannaimperia.com

**Red Rock Threads/
Guttermann**
150 S. Hwy 160, Ste. 298
Pahrump, NV 89048
guttermanthread.com

Habu Textiles
135 W. 29th St., Ste. 804
New York, NY 10001
habutextiles.com

Imperial Stock Ranch Yarn
92462 Hinton Rd.
Maupin, OR 97037
imperialyarn.com

Jagger Spun
PO Box 188
5 Water St.
Springvale, ME 04083
jaggeryarn.com

Jojoland International
5615 Westwood Ln.
The Colony, TX 75056
jojoland.com

**Knitting Fever/Louisa
Harding Yarn/Malibrigo**
PO Box 336
315 Bayview Ave.
Amityville, NY 11701
knittingfever.com

Koigu Wool Designs
Box 158
Chatsworth, ON
Canada N0H 1G0
koigu.com

Lorna's Laces
4229 N. Honore St.
Chicago, IL 60613
lornaslaces.net

Louet North America
3425 Hands Rd.
Prescott, ON
Canada K0E 1T0
louet.com

Mango Moon Yarns
308 W. Main St., Ste. 303
Owosso, MI 48867
mangomoonyarns.com

Mountain Colors
PO Box 156
Corvallis, MT 59828
mountaincolors.com

North Light Fiber
PO Box 1382
Block Island, RI 02807
northlightfibers.com

Plymouth Yarn Company
500 Lafayette St.
Bristol, PA 19007
plymouthyarn.com

Skacel Collection
PO Box 88110
Seattle, WA 98138
skacelknitting.com

**Tahki-Stacy Charles Inc./
Filatura di Crosa**
70-60 83rd St., Bldg. 12
Glendale, NY 11385
tahkistacycharles.com

Trendsetter Yarns
16745 Saticoy St., Ste 101
Van Nuys, CA 91406
trendsetteryarns.com

Supreme Corporation/UKI
PO Box 848
Hickory, NC 28603
supremecorporation.com

Universal Yarn
5991 Caldwell Business Park Dr.
Harrisburg, NC 28075
universalyarn.com

Webs
6 Industrial Pkwy.
Easthampton, MA 01027
yarn.com

INDEX

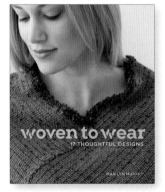
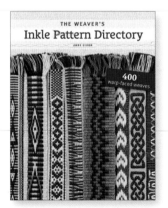